the
ding
dong
diaries
2

jack soliman

Dear Adrienne!
I appreciate you!
Thank you always!

Please
enjoy!

Jack

Most names replaced with initials. If the story involves anything sensitive, or not too "friendly", initials have NO correlation to the actual name.

Details to the best of notes taken. Conversations condensed where practical.

NO favor, compensation or special treatment was asked, or expected of any businesses mentioned.

No pets, people or escrows were hurt during the writing of this book. Feelings? Most likely.

Paperback ISBN-13: 978-0-9985394-2-3
Ebook ISBN-13: 978-0-9985394-3-0
Audiobook ISBN-13: 978-0-9985394-4-7

You made this sequel possible. Unlike the postman who only rings twice, thousands of you have allowed me to ring way, WAY more than twice.

May the titles baffle, challenge, entertain, tickle and mess with your brain, keep some of you wide awake in the middle of the night.

Beyond the joy of gasping and choking on my most profound moments of failure, stupidity and embarrassment, **I hope the warmth, kindness, humor and love of so many shining through the pages puts a smile on your face and heart above all else.**

Jack Soliman
Real Estate Agent
Chino Hills, California

P.S. Well, OK. ALMOST every page. ☺

Foreword

There are real estate agents, and there are real estate agents. Dozens may even come by the name of Jack. But there is only one Jack Soliman. If you know what I mean.

Like many that knocked on my door – agents, salespersons, and missionaries – I gave them my usual please-don't-bother-me attitude. Obviously, Jack wasn't spared from a cold shoulder initially. Pardon me, Jack, but society has programmed us not to open our doors to strangers for reasons of safety.

Through his patience, perseverance and pleasant personality, he graduated from being a neighborhood "pest" (his own word) to becoming a welcome guest, and ultimately to being a friend. If anything, the information he distributes on a regular basis is informative and relevant to every homeowner. To be fair I, too, graduated from being a snob, to being a friend, and now a potential client.

So next time you hear the "ding-dong" chimes or gentle tap on your door, look into your peep hole. If you see Jack, open not only the door to your home but also the door to your heart. Trust me, you won't regret it.

george

George S. Rivera

Chino Hills Homeowner since 1990

Thank You

These two best words will NEVER change.

* * *

If we sold doughnuts, these stories are the unexpectedly tasty sugar-dusted doughnut holes resulting from it.

My giant 10,000+ extended families in Chino Hills, and a few other special spots. THANK YOU for welcoming, laughing with, waving at, trusting, feeding, swearing at, hugging (remember that?), buying with, selling through, referring, defending, licking (not you, your dogs!), messing around with, actually missing, sharing with and shedding tears with me. This heart of mine LOVES and THANKS YOU ALL.

My incredible partner John & I can be two juicy beef patties, but it wouldn't work quite perfectly without buns, cheese, onions and the special sauce. We practically have the rest of the Balsz family — his wife, Michelle; daughter, Lauren and son, Brandon, in our tasty burger beast of an engine firing on all cylinders. To my second family — Love you guys! Thank you! (P.S. John's sister Kim just got licensed too. Who could be next? His dad?)

Rich King, our awesome broker at King Realty, for among other things, suggesting I look into a golf bag carrier to lug my stuff around town, and for letting me test drive his. Even if the Jackbrella never gets baptized, you ARE its godfather. Thank you!

Special thanks to Ramon, who was able to capture the questionable character lurking at his front door for the incriminating cover picture.

Heartfelt gratitude to Mike & Marie, Brandon and Ryan, who generously gave of their time and talent installing doorbells for our seniors. And especially Alvin – you went WAY over the call of duty time and again – THANK YOU!

Hedy, my wife of 34 years, and girlfriend of FORTY - still here for me through thick and thin. Our daughters, Ashley (our son-in-law, Sam and soon-to-be little grandson!), Caitlin and Renee. And our youthful senior 11-year-old beloved pekepoo Cooper, still smiling for free as my car window stickers despite missing six teeth. To my family, I love you x 7.

My God & Savior, Jesus Christ. In such a brutal and competitive business, trusting You know what's best for me, and what's not meant to be, is my greatest source of sanity, peace, contentment and joy. Thank you!

Out Of Sight, But Never Out Of Heart

Every day we have is a gift from God. He alone knows how much we all have.

It's never the right time to find out it's time to say "Goodbye." It's always too soon.

I will miss every one of you at your front door, but you'll always have a spot in my heart. That you have kindly and graciously welcomed me is something I'll always be grateful for and remember.

It has been, and always will be a privilege to have been a part of the priceless canvas of your life, even if I was just a little fleck of paint.

AB AC AG AG AG AH AL AM AM AW BA BB BF BG BG BH BK BK BL BR BR BR BW CC CD CD CH CH CK CL CM CM CN CR CS CS DA DF DF DH DH DJ DJ DL DW EB EG EL EM EM EM EW FA FB FJ GD GG GR GR GV GV GW GZ HH HM IB JA JA JA JB JB JC JC JD JE JG JG JG JH JM JM JM JP JP JR JR JS JT JW JW JW JW KO KP LA LA LB LP LS LS LS LW MA MB MC MD MG MH MH MM MM MN MP MS MT MW NM NS NW PB PB PH PP PR PR PS PS RA RD RF RG RH RH RK RL RM RN RN RN RO RS RW RW RV RV RZ SB SB SD SG SH SH SO SP SP SP SR SV TC TK TM TS TS VF VG VN VN VR WC YR

THANK YOU ALWAYS to you and your family.

Before You Start...

(A) There are PICTURES! They're black and white, but links are provided if you'd like to see them in COLOR.

(B) We even have a few VIDEOS! Haven't figured out how to show that on a paper page, so you get a link & QR code.

(C) 2-books-in-1. Check out the BACK cover, in case you haven't, and come right back. *Ding Dong Diaries 2* hopes you laugh, while our compact insider's guide, *Get A Perm,* also hopes you laugh – all the way to your bank. Both are the result of John & me closing over $278 MILLION by successfully serving Chino Hills families.

Bonus: You can display your book in TWO different ways!

(D) There are puns, intentional typos and hidden messages. That's all I'll say. No further comments. ☺

(E) About the ORIGINAL *Ding Dong Diaries*: You can enjoy Ding Dong 2 as a standalone.

If you never got, don't have, lost, gave away, sold, donated or threw away your original Ding Dong, fear not. Just ask. FREE lifetime warranty, autograph and personal delivery for Chino Hills families, no questions asked.

(F) There's a surprise interactive collaboration that many of you inspired somewhere in this book that I'm excited AND really scared about. ***What did I get myself into?***

Jack's Theory of Relationships

I didn't exactly make it up, but observed it as a consistent phenomenon. But first, a truth I accept as foundational:

"It's ALWAYS Jack's fault."

Jack's Theory Of Relationships

People are overwhelmingly consistent.

The difference in how you treat me is based on your perception of me as it changes over time, for better or for worse.

The very first time we met at your door, I am at best an unexpected interruption, or at worst a total nuisance at a very bad time. So it's NOT your fault. NEVER. It's mine.

The next time you see me, you might move me up the scale a little bit, from 'total stranger' to 'I remember you.' Later down the road, you may even know my name, start a conversation, invite me in, offer me some cold water on a 100-degree day. Or 100-degree water on a really cold day. Some of you even greet me with hugs, while a special few of you prefer to affectionately swear at me.

With time, I am treated differently, because you view me differently. And whatever that may be, I accept it.

For the moments that make me the absolute last thing you need to see, I sincerely apologize.

* * *

The choice of taking the blame for everything, while superficially not appealing, is positive and powerful in application. It's not some mental game. It's basic courtesy, considering what I do. Even the nicest of you have bad days. And because it's always my fault, it's never yours. For the occasional truly mean person, I just let it go. There are so many more kind people out there.

*

(If all the above sounded familiar, it's because I practically plagiarized myself from the original. I think it's a fitting reminder as I take you all along this one-of-a-kind neighborhood crawl. Again.)

See that email above?

I'd really love to hear from YOU.
Anything you'd like to say. Good, bad, anything.

But NOT now.
<u>AFTER</u> you read it would be better.

P.S. Please feel free to dog ear or scribble
anywhere and everywhere.

January 3

Puppy Eats Sheet

As F welcomed me in, she says she has an incredible story for me.

"You'll never believe this, Jack. So sorry the house is in a mess. I had no idea where that beautiful note you wrote me went.

Two weeks ago, we got two new little puppies. This morning, one of them had THIS in his mouth!

That's how we were able to find your number and contact you."

Nice job, smart, little Winston!

Jackddd.com/Winston

* * *

THANK YOU, F. You and R have always been so kind to me.

Butternut Squash

Two months into her listing with her friend, Z calls, a little discouraged and disappointed. Her words:

"I got the "friend's discount." But I didn't realize it meant discount everything: pictures, marketing, follow-up, service and motivation. When can we meet?"

DISCLAIMER: It is absolutely UNETHICAL for any agent to solicit a listing that is active, on hold, or withdrawn. The only time it is legal is when it either expires, or is cancelled ON the Multiple Listing Service.

It is NOT unethical for an agent to receive such a call provided it is initiated by the SELLER.

We got together. John & I discuss a game plan, and answer all her concerns and questions. In days, it is back on the market. No, not with us, but with her same friend.

For dessert, we get accused of soliciting her business. Fortunately, Google Voice never forgets anything, and saved both transcript and the actual voice message, with date stamps, so even my great-great grandkids can listen to it.

Can you blame me for feeling like a nut who got buttered before getting squashed?

January 13

Adopted

"Hello, Jack. We are relocating ... would like your advice about plans to sell our home. Do you have time to come and meet with us tomorrow afternoon? We ... have been impressed with the info you have passed out in the neighborhood."

She also said, "Not sure if you remember who we are..."

"Are you the ones with the three collies, and the cat who thinks he's one of them?" I asked, after shaking my brains.

"Haha, you got the right family! They're Shelties, but yes!"

Did the Shelties adopt the cat? Did the cat adopt the Shelties? P & M told me they're really a well-adapted family.

Jackddd.com/adopt

* * *

P & M, THANK YOU so much for thinking of us, and wishing you the most exciting adventures ahead!

In so many ways, a ton of you have adopted me, like taking in a lost puppy. (Well, more like an old stray.) What touches me the most is you had to CHOOSE to do it. That makes me special.

Fifty Shades Of Grrr...

I've seen signs warning me of vicious dogs, angry owners, even one of 'Very Angry Owner AND Dog.'

Having heard colorful language that's anything but grey, and received the whole spectrum of anger, from very mild irritation to ballistic outbursts, I am careful.

Jackddd.com/wifi

Walking up T & S's front steps, I know I'm NOT scared of WiFi.

So I bravely continued until I got closer.

Oh.

Forget WiFi.

The sign actually read -

BEWARE OF WIFE!

* * *

Kidding aside, S is one of the nicest ladies in town. T is alright too.

January 15

Heart Attach

Standing at the door was J & A's granddaughter, an adorable little girl named E. She was just two when I first met her.

Over the years, it got to the point where her grandma couldn't even talk to me unless E went first.

"Hi Jack! Let me show you how to play this thing. Me first. Then you. OK?" Of course, I lost. Every single time.

The time came to say goodbye to J & A. I hoped to catch E one last time. But not knowing what time anyone was going to be home threw me in a bit of a time-sensitive dilemma.

Happily, A called later, saying J was already in their new place getting things ready, and she just got home. She asked if I could swing by after 7 PM, as E would be there.

"Jaaaaaaacck!" E excitedly greeted me by the front door.

She brings me up to speed on her ballet lessons, and tries showing off her handstand. We settled by the staircase, as the house was almost empty. I checked with A, and asked E,

"Hey, E, can we take a selfie?" What a ham. Like a pro, she just posed, smile in place. Click!

Without missing a beat, she yanks my camera from me. "Now it's MY turn. I will take the selfie," said E.

I then told her to always continue growing to be the smart young lady her future is waiting for her to become.

As we hugged one last time, it brought back a moment that will always live in the most tender part of my heart.

*

On this one visit, E raised her little arms high, and said, "I'm taller than you! I'm taller than you!"

Hmmm. I bent my knees a little bit, "Almost?"

"I'm taller than you!"

I finally scrunch down on my knees, hunch my back a bit, and told her, "I think you REALLY are taller than me now, E! Look!"

A is standing right behind her, watching all this and smiling. Before I knew it, I felt two little stubby arms wrapped tightly around my neck, her little face squished in. And she stayed there for quite a few moments.

"Awww, you little sweetie pie!" I whispered, my eyes welling up, my arms wrapped around her.

"She loves you, Jack," A gently said.

On my way home that night, the rain drops kept falling. I wasn't alone. The clouds were crying too.

* * *

J & A, THANK YOU for sharing your precious little E with me. You guys are so blessed. Miss you all, many happy years in your new spot. Please give E a bunch of hugs and kisses for me.

January 17

In-and-Out, What's This All About?

Their sign welcomes me in

I'm greeted with a smile

Looking forward to meat

A smile, and my order is counterside

Burger in hand, I'm on my way

Few things more iconic than In-N-Out

That's what a hamburger is all about

Her son welcomes me in

I greet with a smile

Looking forward to meet

No smile, and I'm ordered curbside

Flyer still in hand, I'm sent away

Few things more ironic than in-and-out

When this door knocker is shown out

* * *

She wasn't asking, "Where's the beef?" But she definitely found a beef. With me.

Oh, sorry. Different burger.

(American) Sign Language

Many of you have greeted me while on your phone. So begins an interesting exchange of hand signals and facial expressions.

E: Chatting on the phone, smiles, raises his eyebrows to acknowledge me.

Me: I mouth, "Hi, E! So sorry," without a sound, exaggerating my mouth movements, as if it helps.

E: Uses his free hand to point to the phone.

Me: "Enjoy!" I silently say, as I hand him the latest newsletter.

E: Nods, as he grabs my flyers.

Me: "Thank you," silent movie style. I also wave both my palms at him as I leave.

E: Smiles as he closes door. (Mind you, he's holding a simultaneous conversation with someone else.)

* * *

From family and school, I learned to speak English, Mandarin, Hokkien (our local Chinese dialect), passable Tagalog and enough Spanish to order at King Taco. Lengua and cabeza, anyone?

*From door knocking, I've cobbled together a fusion of sign language and pantomime – the OTHER ASL - **Accidental** Sign Language.*

January 18

That's inSAME!

When I first met Jake, I told him that's the name my dad went by.

"Is that right?" he asked.

My dad's real name is Joaquin.

"No way," he said, "that IS my real name too!"

What a coincidence. Then Jake threw another whopper my way.

"Been calling you Jack all these years. I finally saw your real name in the fine print, Joaquinito!"

He pronounced it perfectly, of course.

Then he tells me, "Did you know when I was a child, my name was actually Joaquinito? I'm sure you know it means 'little Joaquin.' My dad told me to chop it once he felt I was a grown man. That's why my legal name is Joaquin. Had I kept it, the two of us would be Joaquinito!"

Insane how our name can be that same.

My Heart's Not On My Sleeve

The problem with my face, aside from missing good-looking genes, is it doesn't hide anything: zits, craters and feelings.

When I saw Y, she asked if I knew they were in default.

"No, Y. I'm afraid to see families I know. I'll feel bad, and whatever I feel or think will be written all over my face."

She shared what they're going through, and how they are in the process of resolving it.

"But we're getting attacked every day by agents sending letters, emails, calling us. Some even show up and coldly tell us to sell now. It's stressful enough. You're never like that. And if we ever did anything, there's no way I'd want to work with any of them. I would only call you."

"Y, so sorry to hear that. I'm glad you're able to fix it. You know, we've been in your shoes. In the mid '90s, the company I sold insurance for cut my commission by almost 90%. We were THAT close. Never forgot the guy parked in front of our home every few weeks snapping a picture, hired to make sure the house wasn't getting thrashed just in case we lost it."

* * *

To all our families whom John & I have served through the most difficult of personal circumstances, THANK YOU for trusting us, and knowing we will see you through with the utmost privacy, care and compassion.

January 22

Nixed Nextdoor

Filling out listing paperwork, S says, "Hey – did you see what happened to you on Nextdoor? Here, check it out. I'll send you some screenshots later."

First post didn't bother me. The poster just wanted someone to call the cops on me. (Now why does THAT sound familiar?) Not that I didn't care, but because no matter what I do I can't please everybody. ***My sincerest apologies to the poster.***

Scrolling through comments, I felt myself going quiet, and squinting just a little harder. Tried really hard, but failed.

My finger wasn't enough so my hanky came to the rescue.

S went, "By the time I responded there were already lots of posts. Jack, you know you are loved by our families here, and we weren't gonna let him pick on you."

Some responses were little short stories.

* * *

To so many of you, in my absence, who speak up for and defend me, my heart (& tear ducts) are filled with gratitude.

(Screenshot collage on the next page)

Realtor

It's a guys the jack realtor butther and pushing to sell the property and chino Hills to Asian people for cash please report this people to police o the city thank you

Posted on 29 Oct to

 M Oct 29

Jack is a reliable, honest realtor who works to help residents buy or sell homes. He has an impeccable reputation with the neighbors of We've known him for years.

☺ 3 Thanks

R Oct 29

WTF does this mean?

☺ 1 Thank

S Oct 29

Jacks seems to be a friendly realtor. If Chinese people have cash money than he will sell to them. Police won't do any thing. Jack is not doing anything wrong. Just selling property to make his commission.

☺ 2 Thanks

S Oct 29

you might want to clarify your statement. Jack has been nothing but courteous and respectful in all my interactions with him.

☺ 2 Thanks

Oct 29

There's nothing illegal about that. Jack is an upstanding individual who is highly supportive of this community.

☺ 2 Thanks

J Oct 29

Jack is really kind! Even though we don't need a realtor or plan on selling, I actually enjoy him coming by every so often to say hi!

P Oct 29

Jack has a huge heart and does a lot of nice things for many in our community outside of his business. He prides himself on knowing most of our names which is pretty impressive for anyone. Don't take his friendliness as annoying as he has put in a lot of work to sell homes here in Chino Hills for many years. He is also a resident and sells homes to and for every race.

☺ 4 Thanks

 J Oct 29

Jack is a really nice realtor. He is very professional- we don't plan on selling, but he keeps us informed on our neighborhood. He's a hard worker in this heat! When he heard that I was hospitalized, a week later I found a beautiful plant on my porch from him. Nice guy.

☺ 2 Thanks

K · Oct 30

Please do NOT report Jack to the police. He is very personable and takes the time to get to know our neighborhood. If he bothers YOU, use his contact information and leave him a message kindly asking him not to visit your home anymore. The interest he takes in getting to know us gives me hope that if one of us does decide to sell, he might be putting that same effort into finding us good future neighbors. If he works half as hard at selling homes and finding homes for his clients as he does marketing himself, then I imagine him to be an excellent realtor. The police are for reporting suspicious activity and keeping our neighborhood safe. Not for reporting things that bother us. Jack is neither

January 23

Honey I (Almost) Sold The Kids!

One of our little but powerful extras for our families who are selling is pre-marketing their homes.

Part of it includes me taking a few pictures.

But something caught my eye – and zooming in, there he was. M & M's mischievous toddler was making faces right through the front wrought iron gate.

It was fun teasing them – as I sent them the shot and told them to just take a good look, making sure they were fine with it. Took a few minutes before I got the call back.

"Jack, is that my little boy??"

Of course, we didn't use THAT one.

* * *

Thank You, M & M, for the privilege of serving you.

While the title is meant to be funny, it is no laughing matter – unless specifically excluded by customary regulation or intent, the buyer has the right to have anything captured in the photographs included in the sale.

Of course their son would be excluded, but on at least two occasions, attempts were made to include a mother-in-law WITH the sale of the house. For a DISCOUNT.

Three Funerals And Maybe A Wedding

Having just visited them, I couldn't believe the news this very kind and grand lady had passed away.

Her son was getting ready to fly back, for her eulogy and her memorial, when he, too, unexpectedly passed away.

So tough to see the broken heart of a husband losing his wife, and see it so soon crushed again, a father grieving for his son.

Not even two months pass and I receive details of his service.

Married for seventy years, everyone on their street knew this couple had a 9 AM donut date every day. I have wonderful moments with them tucked deep in my heart.

Their son, whom we lost way too soon, and their daughter-in-law, I knew them well, too. They always had a kind smile, held in place by their big, warm and gracious hearts.

On my way out after the third memorial, their granddaughter approached me, and said,

"Jack, we have to stop meeting like this."

She shared the next time the family gathered together, it might be her wedding.

* * *

With precious memories in their hearts, I wish this beautiful family many moments overflowing with joy in years to come.

January 29

ICU

Not the usual place with nurses and doctors buzzing among beeps and clicks. In many ways, our homes should be an intensive care unit – lots of love and care for our families.

Having never met Mr. A face-to-face, his wife, B, shared he was one who was very protective of his family. As a husband and father of three daughters, I can relate, and absolutely respect him for doing so.

Over the years, the following scenario repeated itself:

Walking up to their front door, I'd ring their camera doorbell.

The now-familiar gravelly voice would matter-of-factly say,

"Hi Jack, you can leave it there."

"Sounds good, Mr. A. Please say 'hello' to B. Thank you!"

He could have easily ignored me. I would have never known.

I can almost guess what he'd say when I made my visits to their front door...

"I see you."

* * *

For always taking the time to greet me, THANK YOU, Mr. A. It will always be a privilege to have served your family. B, may our Lord bless all of you with many years filled with love and joy, happy grandkids and not too much humidity!

Cries Cream

C called, telling me her husband, I, had passed away unexpectedly. Nothing ever prepares me when any family shares news like that. And I was just looking forward to meeting him soon.

Their family was very close, even among the nephews and nieces, who had wonderful relationships with her husband.

One afternoon I got a text from C.

Attached was a picture of her with her sons, nephew and niece, huddling with smiles, each with a cup or cone of ice cream in their hands.

It made me smile.

But I never thought ice cream could make me cry too.

* * *

C, my deepest sympathies on I's passing.

I am touched that you would share such a difficult, yet beautiful moment with me. THANK YOU.

February 3

Feast Of Three Rings

I'm definitely no baby Jesus, but on this special day I felt like royalty brought me some precious gifts.

Didn't get a visit from three kings, but got notifications from two kings and a queen. It's the 21st century, after all!

2:35 PM: A lady called for me to list her home.

3:00 PM: A text message says we're getting paid.

4:17 PM: Another call came in for a new seller.

All on the same afternoon within a two-hour period. Blessings over which I not only had no control, but had no idea it was going to happen, or even thought were remotely possible.

How remote? I hope to see flowers where I've seeded, nurtured and watered. This trilogy of blooms sprouted from spots I never even planted in.

These were gentle rays of sunlight shining through a thick busy forest of a hectic afternoon.

Sometimes, lighting strikes thrice.

You'll Never Find Them

Well, that's how that conversation started.

A came over, and shared that his neighbors moved a few years ago out of the area, but decided to lease their home out.

"However, we're still very good friends. I'm still in touch with them, and they're actually thinking about selling. You're a hardworking nice guy, so let me give you their contact info, and you can tell them I asked you to get in touch with them."

Thank you, E & R, for having us take care of selling your home. Despite everything getting done by phone, text and email, it was so nice to have 'met' you all.

* * *

I could never have seen that one coming.

Having taken care of so many referrals, the ONE thing that motivates (and in a good way, frankly terrifies) me, is that with the obvious responsibility of doing our very best to help someone buy or sell a home, we've been also entrusted with a cherished relationship between the referrer and the referred.

THANK YOU so much, A, and to so many of you who have counted on us to serve your friends and loved ones.

February 8

Peek-A-Pooch

Niki is G's very sweet maltepoo.

As we were chatting at the door, she runs out. And then she plants herself by my car, in front of our pekepoo, Cooper.

More like in front of a STICKER of Cooper, who appears to be looking out from behind the window.

She paces excitedly around my car, even perching right on to get a closer look. And just waits there for a while.

Pretty soon the neighbors are having a good time watching her do this. Always look forward to seeing Niki, and River, who went from rambunctious to model doggie.

One of my all-time favorite moments.

* * *

Cooper stickers were replaced in 2019. New ones are pretty lifelike. It's fun when I take him out for a ride with the windows down, ears flapping in the wind, flashing his underbite, and watching people do a double take and smile.

More color pics at:
jackddd.com/niki

Spelling Been

The last time I was in a spelling bee was sixth grade. That qualifies me a has-been.

Getting your name correctly spelled is one compulsive and lingering consequence of those days.

I've learned there's Michelle or Michele.

There's Tere, Teri, Terri, Terry, and Terrie. A mistake here would be … Terri-ble!

Jon or John?

Even Jennifer could go one 'n' less as Jenifer, or Jinnefer.

Who knew Cynthia can be spelled with the 'y' and 'I' trading places?

Hearing her name, I calmly responded like a seasoned barista offering endless options:

"Would that be an 'f' or a 'ph'?"

'Ph' she said.

"So nice to meet you, Stephanie," I said, thanking her.

Until I found out later that name needs a second question: "Would you like that with an 'e' or without?"

Because hers ended with just an 'i,' NOT 'ie.'

i.e., Stephani.

Or, to 'e,' or not to 'e.'

February 9

> *** WARNING: RATED PG, sort of. There's a four-letter, adult word.**

Pink Light District

For me, the best cup of coffee in town belongs to the Dirty Penguin, back then always bathed in shades of pink. Taylor, who started that place, calls me early one morning, telling me the audiobook guy is here today.

"So Jack – what do you do?" asked Joe.

Before I could answer, Taylor cut in, with his usual excited and loud voice blasting across the café:

"Oh, he's a local celebrity! He's a porn star!"

And with that, he sucked the air out of me, and out of everyone else sipping their flat whites. You could hear a coffee bean drop.

With all eyes on me, and nowhere to hide, he waves at everybody and calmly said:

"Just kidding, everyone. He's only a great real estate agent."

I've NEVER been more embarrassed.

* * *

It's under new ownership as of August, 2020. WOW. Did not expect their coffee could taste even better.

@DirtyPenguinCoffeeCo
14708 Pipeline Avenue, Suite C, behind Roscoe's

Quinceañera

Always a joy to see S & V. And their little buddy, Charlie. He has to be one of the sweetest Chihuahuas in town, one of the few who never barked much at me from day one.

"Jack, not sure you know, but S passed away 4 months ago. I thought you should know. S always enjoyed your company."

V was visibly shaken. I can't believe what I just heard.

"And then there's little Charlie. He was going to throw him a quinceañera. But now I don't know. You think I should?"

"If you don't mind me saying, I think that would be fun for Charlie, a great way to keep your mind occupied on something wonderful to do, and a funny and beautiful way to honor S."

Two weeks later we ran into each other at Albertson's.

"Jack, did you get Charlie's card yet? THANK YOU for the candles. We sent you some pictures too."

* * *

S, so hard to realize you're no longer here. THANK YOU always for being so kind to me. You'll always have a spot in my heart.

jackddd.com/charlie

February 10

Effective Objective Perspective

As we took their listing, J told us about the difficult decision they had to make.

"Well, there's my old buddy X. He's the broker I told you about who sits in his office and complains he doesn't have any business. But then there's my sister-in-law, N's sister."

Oh. Double Oh.

"So here's what we're going to do. Our sister-in-law will help us buy our retirement home, but we will list with you. Remember my son, G? He spent forty-five minutes on the phone convincing N & I we should go with you. He said:

'Mom, Dad. This isn't about friends or family. It's about your biggest financial asset. Dad, don't you already have that local agent you like talking to, that you tell me about? I love Aunt Y, but she's way out of your area, and isn't even really active anymore. I strongly encourage you to pick the local expert for something like this. And you already got one. Just call him.'"

* * *

G, THANK YOU for your support, and for casting a vote for us. J & N, we'll always be grateful for the privilege of serving you!

John & I are keenly aware just how many agents most people know, from friends to family members and everything in between. The choice is always yours, and we are always grateful for every one of you who have trusted us to serve you.

* WARNING: RATED R, for Historical Violence.

Hearts & Chocolates

Just before Valentine's, John & I were sent something startling. It didn't contain any hearts or chocolates, but it was filled with unfounded accusations. They were upset, because the new buyers had the money to fix up their old house.

Happy VIOLENTine's Day to us!

*

Weeks later, we received a very nice note from them. Thankfully, they realized how hard we fought in negotiating an **extra $65,000 MORE** for them, over an exact home in slightly BETTER condition than theirs that closed about the same time.

* * *

THANK YOU SO MUCH for hearing us out, working past your emotions, and seeing the facts of what we did for you.

John & I NEVER give up on any of our families, no matter what anyone, or even they themselves, may say or do.

(For the few weeks that we lived with their misunderstanding, it still felt like Valentine's. Not the warm and fuzzy American kind we're used to. More like the Aztec variety. They loved chocolate. And they loved hearts too. Especially those they yanked out of other peoples' chests.)

February 14

Metamorphosis Meets Murphy's Law

Metamorphosis reminds me of butterflies - a transformation with some squeezing and pain, but goes from ugly to pretty.

Murphy's Law. Things CAN always get worse...

After six years, they were ready to list. They asked a lot of questions, and filled pages of their yellow pad. At the last moment, they informed us they weren't quite ready after all, and would be in touch in a month or two.

John & I are never the pushy kind. We thank them for their time, and ask them to reach out for anything else.

Not a WEEK later, their home is for sale. At the price we recommended. It was an agent who sold one home three years before.

With a clearly NON-SOLICITOUS text, I wished them the best, asking what we could have done better, or even apologize for.

Can you imagine standing in front of Mr. Rogers, to find out too late it's really Mike Tyson winding up to punch you out?

"Oh, we went with our son's friend. He's like a son to us! Since he's really new and doesn't do a whole lot, could you give us the people you use to do a few things for us? You are truly a friend indeed!!"

Didn't see any butterflies, but felt stung by a few bees.

That's metaMURPHYsis!

February 16

Race Hoarse

I can't recall ever running a race. But my vocal chords have.

It was about 6:30 PM as we got ready to record the audiobook for Ding Dong #1. Joe and his partner Randy explained how the whole process worked, suggesting we break the whole book down into three sessions of two hours each.

As I read each page, Joe & Randy would follow, flipping along as I went.

My biggest regret?

There were moments when Joe laughed loud enough, and they'd simply draw a circle in the air, a signal for me to just do the page over.

The snickering was edited out of the final cut.

The next time I do this, all the bloopers STAY.

It was past midnight when my raspy voice finally galloped past the finish line more than six hours later.

*The audiobook for Ding Dong #1 is available, and Ding Dong #2 is in the works. Please feel free to check out the Ding Dong store at **DingDongDiaries.com**, or scan this QR code.*

February 16

Clothes Encounters Of The Third Kind

From your perspective, I realize my visits are completely unannounced and unexpected at best, and sometimes flat out inconvenient at the worst possible times.

I've never detained any of you with a long, drawn out spiel, or God forbid, a hard-core sales pitch. I'm content to say "Hello," happy to see you all doing well, and off I go.

Of course, all bets are off if YOU drag me in, stuff me into your couch, and make me answer as many questions as you have.

Out of respect for you, my visits are often brief encounters.

But over the years, a few also decided to make them brief encounters –

because it was all they had on.

Jackddd.com/brief

* * *

Been asked a few times how long I can keep talking if they let me. Twenty-four hours would not be hard at all with minimal care and feeding. I think I can beat Scheherezade's 1,001 Nights. I got pictures, videos and stories from 100,001 Visits.

Tears For Ears

"Great job on selling (neighbor to left)'s house!"

"Would it worth doing (this)? Or should we do (that)?"

"Someone I haven't heard from in twenty years got licensed now calls me monthly. I told her we already have a local expert we've grown to like, trust and will sell with. That's you."

"That was a great price you got for (neighbor to the right)!"

"The neighbor behind me has these trees that cover our view. You think you can talk to them for me?"

"Can you make the search for our next home for these specific models only?"

"Man, sorry to hear you lost that future seller just for asking about the trees. Don't worry. We're yours when it's time. Already told you we're selling and buying with you, Jack."

"Just told (another neighbor's son), 'Make sure to call Jack. He's known your mom for years, and sells the most here."

"Jack, can't believe (said neighbor) got an agent I never heard of, didn't price it correctly, and cost them at least $70,000!"

*

"Uhh...we went with another agent for our purchase, who will also list our home."

* *

I must admit those words ending an almost seven-year journey felt like vinegar pouring into my ears.

We NEVER dare presume to have earned your business, until everything is signed AND closed. This was the closest "sure thing," if there ever was one, not because I thought so, but because of X's repeated promises.

Turns out he "heard" things I never said, and "heard" words the other agent never uttered. His fists didn't knock me out. His ears DEAFeated me, twice in a row.

* * *

Age and wisdom have taught me to be simpler. There are only two kinds of problems in life: Those I can fix, and those I can't.

Simple doesn't mean I don't get frustrated. I focus on what I could have done better, or what can be learned. And when I'm really smart, I ask God if He's trying to teach me something.

While it's true we can't drive forward staring at the rear view mirror, hindsight is 20/20, and is worth an introspective look when we find ourselves safely stopped at life's red lights.

It's easy to be thankful when it's obvious, or hopeful when we're looking to the future. It's harder to be grateful when we have to slow down, pause and take a few steps backward.

Took more than a week before I even realized He sent me two exams for the price of one.

Quiz #1: For 2,413 days, it seemed things were going my way. In one afternoon, it all went away. "The LORD gave, the LORD has taken away; Blessed be the name of the LORD."

Indeed, death and taxes are still the only "slam dunks" in life.

Quiz #2: You likely read right through it like I lived right through it.

Thumb back a few pages to February 3 for AFTER-the-fact details that made my jaw drop. My turn to be hard of hearing.

*2:35 PM: This listing was in the exact neighborhood where I'd find out X dropped me a few days **LATER**. And I have only seen her once in the last ten years.*

3:00 PM: We gave up on this early on. 99% of the time this would have never happened.

4:17 PM: This seller was an active broker, someone I never expected, with a home up the street from X.

A Biblical truth I love (and have a hard time with) teaches that only when I am weak can God show Himself strong.

*When I'm most confident, He gently reminds me who's in control. It's never me. But in my lowest moment, He practically replaced in **ADVANCE** what I was about to lose three days later, and added a bonus just because He can.*

That's 'gracious' in the strongest sense – a gift undeserved, and not the result of anything I've done. He owes me nothing. He didn't have to, doesn't have to, but chose to anyways.

Just like He gave us all His Son.

February 19

Dogs...

Bark. Well, that happens all the time.

Bite. A couple of times were nips. Only one time did I become an unsuspecting blood donor.

Leave dog hair. As I like to say, if I end the day without a strand of dog hair, good chance NOTHING happened that day.

Poop. Let's just say I've spent an afternoon trying creative ways to scrape off the unpeanut butter without having to touch it.

Happy. Got hundreds upon hundreds of pictures with your doggies and their smiles.

Happee. Some are SO excited to see me, I've been lightly sprinkled at least three times. That's a badge of honor for me.

And lastly... As H opened their front door, their little buddy, who was getting up in years, waddled up next to me, and decided to sneeze on my pants.

H apologized, and offered to get something to wipe it off.

"Oh, don't even worry about it," I said.

"'Snot' a big deal."

Jackddd.com/dogs

P.S. That's our Cooper, who wasn't harmed, wet nor flushed.

* WARNING: RATED R. Very mature topic of suicide.

You Won't Feel A Thing

The more I wrestled with whether or not to include this, the more I felt I should. This needs to be said.

Over the years, many of you have opened much more than your front doors. You opened your hearts, and allowed me a window into your happiest, but at times most difficult chapters of your family's life.

One conversation took an unexpected turn that jolted me.

"We live in a cruel world. It's not a bad way to go. It's just 'stepping off.' You won't feel a thing."

I'm so glad this person's OK. But it doesn't always end well.

And this isn't the only time something like this was shared.

Our tightly-knit community has not been spared of this. If you or a loved one ever need help, please call 909-393-7100, press 1 for a pastor, or call the National Suicide Prevention Hotline at 800-273-8255. Both are 24/7.

A local group dedicated to ending teen suicide you can support is *facebook.com/HangSuicide*. All of you who know, let's keep praying.

February 23

I'll Set Her Straight

Sometimes, it takes adversity to find out who's on your side.

When our family went through a devastating time, some we thought were "friends to the end" joined the stabbing party. But we were blessed by others who came alongside us.

John & I take full responsibility for what we do, every success, and especially, every failure.

But where we run out of words to express our gratitude, is every time one of you have told us of a friend, who is about to sell, or choose another agent, and you take it upon yourself, like M, and tell me, "I'll set her straight."

So many of you have done that for us.

The outcome is so far overshadowed by your gracious and caring words and actions that have ranged from hardcore reasoning to teasing threats.

When we end up losing a listing here or there, you'd come right out, and tell me,

"So sorry you didn't get that listing. You absolutely deserved it. They really should have gone with you. No worries, you know you got ours, OK? Just make sure you take care of yourself and stick around."

So speechlessly thankful for every one of you.

It's A Smile World After All

The only reason why I haven't been blinded after being told so many times I'm a ray of sunshine, is because I've also been told to go where the sun don't shine.

So I cruise on along, a happy shade of cloudy.

Despite my abundant exposure, if not overexposure, to your kindness, I'm amazed I'm not radioactive yet.

Catch you happy? Smile.

Catch you busy? Many of you still smile.

Catch you coming home? Smile.

Catch you on the way out? Wave and smile.

Catch you on the phone? Silent smile.

Catch you not feeling well? You've still smiled.

Catch you after right thigh surgery? S still gave me a smile!

Catch you on a bad day? Lots of you tell me so, and still meet me with a smile.

We all know life isn't a stroll through an amusement park.

But I'm grateful so many of you are the reason why Chino Hills IS my "Happiest Place."

February 25

Triple Frown

Thirteen horses are Triple Crown winners. But one donkey lost all three.

As dedicated local agents, part of keeping up-to-date is reviewing what's happening on the Multiple Listing Service.

But it's more than an info sheet. For us, it's also a score board.

Hmmm. Lost not one, not two, but three in a row, in one day.

I just 'won' the Triple Frown. But the racing gods weren't quite done with me yet.

My sister and brother-in-law live half a planet away, in Irvine. She calls me, saying, "You're not going to believe this! I met Z! When she said 'Chino Hills,' I asked if she knew you. 'Why of course! Jack's amazing! Your brother is the best!'"

What Z forgot to tell my sister was, "And we called another agent." (No, I didn't tell her. Nobody in Irvine is reading this.)

There was a new record. A first-ever Quadruple Clown "winner." The donkey's name? 91709 Jackass, who was appropriately jockeyed by - Jack S.

If it looks like a Jack S, runs like a Jack S, and has a name like Jack S, it MUST be Jack S.

P.S. He never quit galloping. Some disliked him enough and changed the "Jack" into "Bad."

I'm Not Calling Jack

Over the hundreds of listings we have taken in Chino Hills, there are THREE ways families have gotten a hold of us:

- By phone (the most popular);
- By text (becoming the most popular);
- By email (works just fine).

*(Want a useful CRAZY tip? My cell number, **909-262-3132** can be easy to remember, IF you remember how to remember it.*

*My email, **jack@91709jack.com** is much easier to keep in mind. Did you know you can enter any email, as though you were texting it? It works like a charm. Try it - just not thousands of you at the same time.)*

On my way down from our new listing on this one street, C was busy at his front yard as always. Rolling my window down, I yelled "Heeeeeeeeyy, C!" as I drove by.

Moments later, in my rearview mirror, I see C in the middle of the street, animatedly waving jumping jacks.

I swung around, and stopped at his home.

"Wait till the neighbors hear about this. They all even volunteered to call you for me. 'Nah,' I said. 'You watch – I'm gonna WAVE him down one of these days. They all laughed.'"

Not anymore. In honor of C, you can contact us a fourth way:

- By waving me down (THANK YOU so much, C & J!)

February 27

A Chomp & A Chum

CHOMP! It happened so quickly - front door opens, and as I greeted Grandma, a scary dog (that I've never seen before) LUNGES at my right thigh...instant blood donor!

Dog is snarling, poor grandma is screaming, I'm jump-spin-dancing, blood spraying around like an angry lawn sprinkler from a scene in "Kill Jack." (I WISH there was video of that.)

Actually, Grandma mightily yanked on it, as I skip free after one bite. There's a quarter-of-an-inch open wound, with two other marks to prove I'm almost edible.

*

CHUM! Glad C was home, told him what just happened and ran to their bathroom to check out the damage. I also got to scoop up their sweet little dog Ch in my arms.

Thank you, Ch. I felt so much better already.

Apparently this is NOT the only time that dog has bitten. A neighbor's pet was attacked before, but never reported.

* * *

Update: The Humane Society quarantined the dog, just weeks before we'd be immune to that word. Some punctured pants, an ER visit and some antibiotics later, I'm still here.

For the record, I don't blame them. What canine do? It's a risk a chump like me takes.

Lawless Disorder

(In the real estate compliance system, ethical violations are considered serious. In California, the dedicated enforcers who investigate these offenses are members of a special division within the Department of Real Estate. These are true stories.

Unlike the TV show, "The following stories are NOT fictional and do describe actual persons and events.")

"Z showed up at my door. Said he had three buyers interested in my home. I agreed to 3 private showings - unfortunately that didn't work out and then things kept going from there."

Z left an unstamped note in our client's mailbox, a federally prohibited act, saying, "He had a buyer looking for their very model and area school." When we had it on the market, not once did X show it, much less submit an offer.

In a mass marketing text, Z shows homes he sold, when he represented neither side. Conveniently, the resolution of the images and details are fuzzy. Among his 'sales' were his broker's listings he appropriated as his own.

Z supposedly had several buyers for another seller, and allowed termite repairs, and gave workers unauthorized access to the client's home, without their permission. This family reached out to us shortly.

Please support the honest agent of your choice, and not someone who has zeero regard for ethical business conduct or integrity.

February 27

> *** WARNING: RATED PG, sort of, for the mention of a human body part, thanks to Google Voice's bad hearing.**

Lust In Translation

I LOVE Google Voice, for calls I miss. The biggest timesaver is how it transcribes the messages you leave me.

Not recognizing the number, I quickly glance at the transcription. I laughed so hard, I had to actually LISTEN to it.

Next time we met, I played the message he left me.

Then I showed them the transcription. There are few things in life that can top watching people laugh like nuts.

Oh, 'that'? He actually said 'PEANUTS!'

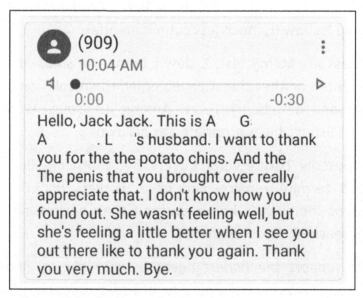

*Keep leaving your messages. Can't wait for Google AI to mess yours up and outdo **this** one.*

Gripes Of Wrath

Seeing an unfamiliar vehicle cruising around this one neighborhood, somehow we caught each other's sight.

"We don't live here. Just driving around to find a home close to ABC school. We can buy first, then sell later."

We talked. And talked some more. "Wow. This is fate! This was meant to be!" They said. It was "love to buy at first sight."

The home must be right for them, and we understand and know it may take a while. It's time well-spent.

Alas, our dates began shriveling. Despite fighting to get five of their offers accepted, they backed out of four of them.

We also got pruned for not showing them our listings. We would, but none of them met THEIR criteria THEY gave us.

Even the home they eventually bought was hanging under the threat of ~~divorce~~ cancellation up to the last moment.

We do not mind the hard work. We signed up for it with eyes wide open. We're THANKFUL for it.

Sadly, our relationship lasted like an eight-month celebrity wedding. We'll probably never know all the raisins why.

Just the same, we are grapeful for the time we spent together serving them, and truly wish them nothing but the best.

Cheers.

February 28

Rad Carpet

Met V once. Forty-seven long months ago. My statistics tell me my chances of running into her were about zip.

As I headed off, I hear,

"Jaaaaaaack!"

The garage door rolls up, and...

"Jack, I follow you. I actually saw you, and chased you down the freeway. I've read your book. I've read your website and all the articles on your flyers. I remember we just met one time. And I laughed because you had put down how many months you haven't seen me. I do not want to be the longest one who's never seen you, so when I saw your umbrella, I said, 'That's Jack! I have to come out!'"

The asphalt I stood on that day felt like a red carpet, as I got treated like a Hollywood A-lister.

I've since met her husband, E, who is just as kind.

* * *

V, THANK YOU so much for the outrageous welcome. I know I'm really nobody famous, but you made me feel like I should get my own star. Not on the Hollywood Walk of Fame. Just my sidewalk, in chalk.

Not to worry. It doesn't take many doors before someone pulls the rug from right under me.

Henry

He's 54 years old. He can be loud.

And always dressed in bright colors.

I know what you're thinking, but I'm not describing myself. (Although I was also 54 at that time.)

That's Henry, R & B's double yellow-headed Amazon parrot.

B takes him out of his cage, and offers to snap a picture of us.

I've gotten pretty good at taking selfies with dogs of all sizes. But a step too close to this beak, and my ear might be a treat.

Just barely a month later, they ask if I saved Henry's pictures.

"Of course, yes, I have all of them."

Made me sad finding out Henry just suddenly passed. I'm glad I met him.

Jackddd.com/henry

* * *

Our dogs, cats, birds and pets aren't just domesticated animals. We love them. Because they're family. We even give them our last name at the vet.

We have family by birth, and family by marriage.

And family by the fact we do pick up their doo-doo.

March 2

Oops! I Did What Again?

Parking my car, my phone rings for a conference call between our seller, John & me. Wrapping up, from the corner of my eye I notice a Chino Hills Police vehicle turn in.

Might as well be a lookie-loo. He cruises by, and from my rear view mirror see him throw a U-turn. Something's happening, and I was probably close to see where the action was.

Before I knew it, it's parked behind ME. With the lights ON.

He comes over, knocks on the window.

"May I see some ID please? We've received a complaint, and you need to leave the premises immediately."

(Not sure what Britney was singing about, but for me, it was SOMEONE else doing "it" again, as in calling cops on me!)

"I'm sorry, officer. What did I do? Been here, legally parked, never got out of the car. Been on the phone last 30 minutes."

"You have to leave."

*

But it wasn't quite the total loss. On the contrary...

"No problem, sir. Umm, may I ask you for a little *favor*?"

I quickly showed him an old picture from my original brush with our local law enforcement seven years ago.

He graciously agreed, and off I went.

* * *

No idea who called the cops. Or why. Had I at least knocked on anyone's door, sure. But I didn't even do Jack, literally. But whoever you are, THANK YOU. You tossed me a sweet lemon.

To every officer who serves and protects us, here in Chino Hills and everywhere else, I appreciate you, and THANK YOU.

What "favor?"

jackddd.com/arrested2

March 2

Twist And Snout

As I sat visiting with S, she gets my attention, and points to the floor.

"Hurry! You got a special treat! Rosie is doing her "happy dance" for you! She rarely does that for anyone!"

I whip out my camera, as S and I couldn't stop laughing as she did her fabulous routine.

THANK YOU, Rosie! You're so adorable!

Rosie and I share something else. We've BOTH been bitten by the same neighborhood dog. I lived to tell my tale, she lived to wag hers.

And her tail, too.

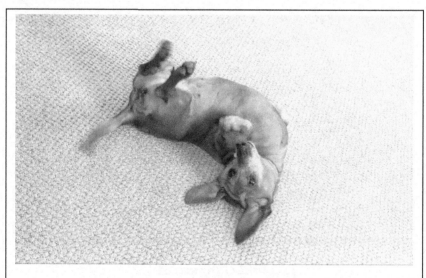

The picture is cute. Wait till you see the VIDEO at Jackddd.com/dance

Charmin' Shepherd

Big dogs usually scare me. My dad raised several to guard our home after dark – they weren't trained to be nice.

One early afternoon a young German shepherd whimpered right up to me with a slight limp. Figured it was still a pup with its folded ears, and paws a bit too big for its legs. And no tags.

It decided to come along with me to a few doors. As I rang the doorbell, it quietly sat to my left, which made it easy to ask the neighbors if it was theirs.

As adorable as it was, sadly no one claimed it, nor even knew to whom it belonged to.

Deciding it wasn't a career for him, my short-term protector and little buddy headed off into the far end of the street...

* * *

(Update: A neighborhood teen was kind enough to go after it. Months later, behind an iron gate, I see a shepherd slowly come over to sniff the flyer I left. He just sat there without a sound. Those eyes looked really familiar. Maybe. Just maybe.)

***More pics at
Jackddd.com/shepherd***

March 6

> *Disclaimer: K is VERY nice, or I would NOT have attempted this, no matter how crazy many of you might think I am.

No SoliciTHIN'

I'm afraid of: heights, dogs that bite, and "No Soliciting" signs.

Some of you have funny, even adorable ones that whisper to me there's someone really nice hiding behind them.

Nothing is more impressive (and irresistible) than a little girl scout going around the neighborhood, and asking you to buy her cookies. That's why I have a soft spot for them, and I love encouraging them to sell me some goodies.

I waited patiently till some Thin Mints became available, and planned for the opportunity to be a sign-abiding* solicitor.

* * *

THANK YOU, K, for allowing me to have a little fun at your expense. You made J, a shy, little girl scout

Jackddd.com/cookies

very happy, and made her giggle telling her the special and almost dangerous mission her cookies were going on.

Technically speaking, I disobeyed the "selling" part. Had she answered the door, it be tempting to ask for five bucks to fulfill the stipulations of her OWN sign. (More details in the picture.)

1989: A Tribute To The O.G.

Can you remember when Peyton Drive had NO stoplights? When many big streets we fly by now didn't even go through? And the only beef patty smell wasn't coming from In-N-Out?

We had never heard of Chino Hills. The map placed it by the armpit of the 60 and 71. One Sunday after church, a kind couple, Jim and Bonnie, invited us over and showed us around town. We felt like we found home.

As a young dad of 25, I was selling life insurance and later, mutual funds, door to door. Before we bought here, we lived in an apartment in Rowland Heights.

Money was tight, so I'd leave home, stay out the whole day, and head back when it was dark. Lunch was usually a PayDay bar. My favorite splurge was the beef barley soup at Denny's.

As I door knocked my way around, I keep running into this jolly character with thick-rimmed glasses and a great personality. He'd tell me, "Hey Jack, forget insurance. Come sell real estate with me." And you never missed him cruising around in his little bright red Mazda Miata with the top down.

His name? Jim Thompson.

At one particular door, an older guy goes, "No, I don't wanna buy anything. But do you wanna buy my house?"

"Well, my wife and I have been looking here..." I said.

"You look like a hardworking young man. Come in, call her!"

I did call my wife, who came with our eldest daughter, who was two then. Our little girl scurried up the staircase, stood by the first room, and exclaimed, "My room! My room!"

John & Monica, the sellers, did us a ridiculous favor. They had planned to price their home at $295,000 the next day.

"We WANT you to buy this home. How much money you got?"

We told them. After huddling in their kitchen, they came out, and said, "The only way you can afford this house is if we sell it to you for $265,000. How's that sound? Got an agent?"

"No. But I know one. May I use your phone?"

I found his number in the yellow pages, and called.

"Hey, Jim, it's Jack, remember me? Hey, we're buying a home. Like now. Can you swing by and be our agent?"

That same night, we opened escrow on 13324 Eagle Canyon Drive. It'll be home for 26 years. Their sign wasn't even up yet.

* * *

As clueless as I was back then, his incredible and consistent work ethic, year after year, when he was ALREADY one of the top agents in town, did not escape me.

Jim, THANK YOU for your magnificent example that you burned into my memory, long before I knew I'd have the honor of following in your giant footsteps a little later into the future. Like twenty-three years later.

I should subliminally blame you for the red Jackmobile too.

Six In The City

We could trace the out-of-area agent's reasoning for listing at $649,000: With NO model matches, the two homes just SIX square feet BIGGER at $650,000 and $638,000 had to do. But:

(1) The slightly bigger model had all 4 rooms upstairs. Most buyers preferred a main floor bedroom AND SHOWER, hence the "ceiling" at $650,000. The smaller home he listed actually had 3 rooms up, but a room & shower DOWNSTAIRS, which is worth more.

(2) While there have not been any recent closings of the smaller plan IN the neighborhood, there was a just-sold model match across the street but AWAY from the tract, at $675,000.

(3) The new listing had even MORE advantages over the $675,000 home, such as: a bigger lot, cul-de-sac location, and was much farther away from the freeway (and associated rumbling tire noise) than the neighborhood comps he used.

We're never for reckless overpricing, but the market at that time was still going up.

Had this been YOUR home, wouldn't you like your agent to actually KNOW your unique property points, to support a listing price between $725,000 and $750,000, giving you room to negotiate?

(As always, EVERY situation is different. Results not guaranteed, but we always give you our best effort!)

March 9

Delivery Boy

It's been over five years since I last saw M. Out of the blue, I get a call asking me to come over.

"Jack, you are literally an answer to prayer! Although I have lots of friends, something told me not to call them.

'God, who am I supposed to call?' In my dream, I mean while I'm asleep, God put your name in front of me!

Next day, I'm having a hard time looking for your number. Then I remembered needing to find some other document for my attorney. And just right under that document, is your *Ding Dong Diaries*, with your info, of course!

If that's NOT a sign, you tell me!"

I'm beyond humbled whenever I've been told I'm an 'answer to prayer.' Just as I do not take that lightly, I don't take myself seriously.

It's a good reminder that it's always GOD who met their request, and I'm just His delivery boy. Better yet, I'm almost like an Amazon package – brown, with a smile at your front door.

* * *

M, so nice to catch up with you, and THANK YOU so much for the very kind words.

Life Imitates Art

Wrestling. Reality TV.

Was I the only one who woke up one day and couldn't believe so much of it is staged? *(Update 2020: And now, Instagram influencers!)*

Every chance I get, I throw Cooper into my car for a carpool buddy.

Actually, I gently scoop him up and plop him on the seat next to me, and turn on the butt warmers for him too.

I just dropped something off, and as I walked back to my car, I couldn't believe my eyes.

Good thing I was quick with my camera hand.

I'll let you decide which one's the real Cooper.

And no, this shot wasn't staged. It's as candid as it gets.

Jackddd.com/double

March 11

Who's At Wahoo's?

"I'd love to meet this Pastor Jack. Heard a lot about him," said the cashier who took my order at Wahoo's.

As I sat to the side waiting to be called, I see THE Pastor Jack walk in with his wife, Lisa. Our Wahoo's has a partition, so people at the counter can't see the customers until they make two little right turns to the cash register.

I scoot over.

"Hi, Pastor Jack. Guy behind the counter said he's never met you, and would love to meet you one of these days." I said.

"Set it up, Jack!" he said.

Right before it was their turn, I went back to the counter.

"Hey, you said you wanted to meet Pastor Jack, right?"

As he nodded, I said, "Tada! Guess who's here!"

* * *

Jack Hibbs pastors Calvary Chapel Chino Hills, and people all over the world know him. On my other Pastor Jack sighting, I didn't even know the home I saw him at was his daughter's, where we had a time for mini-fellowship. Where two or more are gathered in His name, right? Of course, I DO know Jack. Who doesn't?

But I honestly did not expect him to remember this little Jack.

Withering Hates

It's always a treat to be told, "Hey Jack, my parents love you!"

I wasn't quite prepared when someone walked right up to me to say, "Hey Jack, my parents HATE you!"

The other kids around said, "You shouldn't have done that. He might know where you live and who they are!"

As they lingered for a moment, I had a weird hunch.

"Do you live on ABC Street, and your home is maybe about here? And are your parents X & Y?"

The young individual looked stunned, and the friends were of no help as they started cracking up, saying, "No way!!! I told you! I told you! Don't mess with him like that!"

I looked at the young person, and said, "Hey, really, no worries at all. You're good. That is my fault. You go tell your parents I'm so sorry for whatever it is that caused that. Fair enough?"

* * *

The parents have been very nice to me and I'll never say a word. Whatever I did in the beginning that upset them, it is still my fault. The teenager was simply stating a truth in their home, which everyone is free to have – something I have no problem accepting. Just glad I was able to rise a few notches on their welcome scale over the years.

March 12

GPS

J tells me, "I think the house across from me might be selling. Those are the tenants. Have you met the owners, D & R?"

"Actually, no. But THANK YOU so much for thinking of me," I answered. With no contact information, this joined my "Lost and Will Never Be Found" list.

On my way to visit another family One Sunday afternoon, I noticed a few things on the front yard, garage wide open. Something told me to stop. Or more like SOMEONE.

"Hi, just wanted to leave a little update for you..." I said.

"Hi Jack. I'm D," as he quickly goes over our latest flyer.

"Wow. That's impressive. You know, we are selling this home and interviewing agents. Do you have some time now?"

After listing D & R's beautiful home, J said, "Did you know they were only here a few hours sometimes on the weekend?"

"No. I knew my chances of listing their home were zero. I just 'happened' to drive by, saw the open garage, dropped in and said 'hello.' If that wasn't a God thing, I don't know."

To which J agreed, "Amen to that! Good job, Jack!"

* * *

D & R, THANK YOU for letting us serve you. J, THANK YOU for letting me know and being so happy for me. And THANK YOU, God, for always being the 'G' of my GPS, in business and in life.

Fryer & Flyer

"Nothing's defrosted."

That's code from my wife - "the Queen is NOT cooking." Her butler was dispatched to procure Spicy Chicken Sandwiches, from Chick Fil-A, of course. With extra sauce, for the butler.

In the waiting crowd, I thought I saw a familiar face.

"Hi! You look familiar. Are you so-and-so, by XYZ Street?"

"Oh, no. I'm sorry. You got the wrong person," he replied.

As I began to apologize, he goes:

"Wait – Oh you're the real estate guy who's been leaving us notes all these years. We love them! If we ever sell we'd definitely consider you. My name's B, by the way, and there's my wife A. Nice to meet you Jack!"

Something wonderful came out of their fryers.

And something wonderful came of my flyers.

Looks like a Double-Double, but from Chick Fil-A!

* * *

THANK YOU so much, B & A. It was such a treat to meet you both.

March 25

NOTE: I make NO judgment here. X is very nice. I'm the one who shoved both of my feet into my mouth. With that, enjoy another awkward moment.

Boyz II Men*

Garage door was wide open – always a good sign I get to see someone home.

Since I've only met X, I walked up and said:

"Hi! You must be X's son?"

Before I could hand him the latest report and tell him to please tell his parents "I said 'Hello,'" he goes:

"Um, actually, no. I'm X's **boyfriend**."

* * *

Pronounced "Boys to Men," a vocal group from the distant 80s.

Listing Dates

After discussing and answering a homeowner's real estate questions, he turns to me and very matter-of-factly proposed,

"Jack, I know you know a lot of people. If you ever come across someone who is (list of characteristics...), and if they're open to it, would you mind facilitating an introduction?"

Not just once, but twice now.

John had a great suggestion: "You should call it 'Chino Hills Connections!'"*

On the real MLS, the Multiple Listing Service, you can find the listing dates for every property, along with pictures and measurements, and more.

If the MLS were the Marriage Licensing Service, they'd be listing dates. Lots of potential dates, along with pictures and measurements too. What a coincidence!

In all seriousness, while I'm happy to help in any way, this is way beyond my paygrade. But we wish you both, and everyone the very best in your love lives.

* * *

Update: One ended up swiping me to the left. Of course I had to check out who he swiped right for... wouldn't you?

*We're kidding. That's the name of our very active private Facebook group for Chino Hills families. Check it out and join.

April 1

Back For My Future

At about sixteen pounds, my crossbody bag hung from one side of me like two gallons of milk, for hours almost day. I jammed in an inch of heavy cardstock flyers, a cell phone, a big tablet, a Ding Dong or two, fridge magnets, business cards, extra pens, marketing brochures and breath mints. My lower back was really hurting, sometimes keeping me up at night.

I need some THING. Or my back, actually.

It was late night on a perfect day for a foolish idea. I rigged up my old hand cart dolly. Twisting my mind, Velcro and zip ties, it got a bigger file box and an umbrella for shade in no time.

It sort of worked, when it wasn't wobbling off the curb.

Still remember telling my partner John and broker Rich about it at our awards lunch few weeks later. That's when Rich said,

"Hey, I bet you could use a **golf bag carrier** for that!"

Was that a creative moment? Or just another chance for him to prove "All we need is golf?"

In days I checked out his bag carrier. My horse buggy was about to become a Model T.

jackddd.com/thing

WTF!

Close, but not the "World Tchotchke Federation."

It stands for "Wow! That's Freaky!"

There are pictures and stories, no matter how funny, or otherwise, I simply CANNOT put in print for all sorts of reasons.

This goes way beyond some neighbor who might slather a painful coat of color that's a bit off the paint chip charts.

So remember to use the "secret phrase" next time we meet if you'd like a peek:

"WTF!"

You *might* be sorry you asked.

Hahahahaha.

But you never know.

I might show you something Fabulous.

Or Fraudulent.

Or Famous.

Or even Fried.

April 2

Chooseday

As I share this funny picture, I'm just as guilty.

Peyton, the 5th grader who proofread the draft for the original *Ding Dong Diaries* found her share of my typos.

With two daughters in the visual and fine arts, I do love the whimsical colors.

To be sure, the argument could be made for TWO days of the week:

Tuesday or Thursday

Or perhaps it WAS intentionally put up the day before, April Fool's Day, and I fell for it.

That said, this sign was hanging in front of a local SCHOOL.

jackddd.com/chooseday

Zorro, The Masked Hero

In the very early covid days, we were meeting a family who had to be extremely careful due to health reasons.

My wife provided gloves. K kindly provided an N95 mask.

Having never put one on, I instinctively cupped it over my nose and mouth, and pulled the rubber bands over my ears.

K is laughing, and waving his fingers like wipers.

"Not like that. The bottom band goes over your head first."

Now, all I needed was a cape. I was now…

Door-o, The Masked Zero.

* * *

Superhero Bio: Pronounced "DOR-oh." Superman wears glasses. Door-o NEEDS them. Flies around in the Jackmobile. Broke from accepted superhero fashion norms and wears undies INSIDE.

Cop: "Able to drive faster FOR a speeding ticket…"

Wife: "Unwilling to leap from anything tall…"

Door-o: "But I knock-knock and ding dong…"

Chino Hills: "Is it the mail? Is it Amazon?"

"No… It's only Jack. Sigh."

April 4

Why Is Your Face NOT On The Sign?

For years, many of you asked why my face was NOT on the sign. It was answered in Ding Dong #1, May 29 entry, "Facial Recognition."

Early in 2020, there were some new rules about yard signs.

As John & I came out of a particularly tough, but successful listing interview, he turned to me and asked,

"Hey, got something been wanting to talk to you about. Since we have to make changes, you know what would be really awesome? The John & Jack Real Estate Team. What do you think?"

It's really never crossed my mind to want my name or face on a formal sign. Never bothered me a bit, and I understand and respect the fact he & Michelle had invested so much time and resources building their brand, long before we partnered up.

In the dark, it took a split second for me to smile and say "Yes," only because it caught me by surprise, and things like that have a tendency of messing with the lump in my throat.

Anyways, I get a call from S, a very special lady, who used to ask me why my face was NOT on our signs. Now she wanted to know why my face was ON the sign!

* * *

(And what happened to Michelle? – Of course they're still happily married, 37 years and counting!)

miCROSScopic

We've all seen these "He Is Risen" signs, normally no more than knee high as Easter gets closer.

As I walked past this one, it looked HUGE from the middle of the street.

How big is this thing on J & C's yard?

They weren't home, but their daughter C snapped a picture of me next to their homemade custom sign.

Sure felt like I was zapped and shrunk.

Jackddd.com/cross

April 8

Moving Forward

Our meeting with G & G went wonderfully. They weren't ready to sell yet, but were seriously exploring that possibility.

John & I prepare extensively for each of our client meets, everything from facts, figures, marketing, and especially anything that pertains to the uniqueness and desirability of your home in as many ways as possible.

G then says, "Since you were coming, I also prepared something for you. Have a look, and please feel free to do whatever you want with it."

He hands me a plain, unmarked business envelope.

"Go ahead, you can open it now."

As I read it, I'm glad I didn't get any on it.

Some tears moving downward, that is.

I hand it to John, who was wondering why I was crying.

"I hope this gets your sequel moving forward," G said.

Having read the first *Ding Dong Diaries*, he had taken the time and composed a finished, moving foreword for me.

You read it on page 4, reprinted in its entirety.

* * *

George, THANK YOU. That was a hug that came out of left field. Wishing you & G the happiest of years ahead.

Kids Are The G. O. A. T.

Not the ones that bleat with shepherds for parents. I'm talking about the ones with humans for parents.

Your young, and even little ones, who greet me by name.

A few who have answered the door as you parents yell NOT to open for strangers – and they remind you, "But Mom, you and Daddy talk to Jack when he comes here."

The spontaneous gifts of drawings, notes and flower salads.

Even chasing me down to bring me a bottle of water.

"Jack, right? My parents said if I see you to tell you they'll be calling you soon. I think they want to sell this one."

Some have complimented me on my work ethic and marketing, topics which never crossed my mind as a teenager.

"Hey, can you rev your car hard as you pull away?"

"Are you the one with the red car? I still have your book."

To all of you kids, aged two to forty-two, you're the Greatest Of All Time. THANK YOU!

* * *

If you like slow-cooked goat, simmering in a special curry sauce, go to Bombay Blues. Their fire-roasted eggplant mash is amazing too! They were our #1 lockdown takeout.

bombay-blues.com
2545 Chino Hills Parkway, Suites A-C, next to Freshh Donuts.

April 9

Psychic Listing Hotline

It's rare catching J & Y, as they spend all their extra time lounging in their waterside home by the river in Arizona.

Their favorite threat: "One of these days, Jack! One of these days..." No, I've never asked if "THIS was the day."

This one time, Y greets me at the door with a surprised look.

"Did my neighbor K call you?"

"No," I said.

"Did my husband call you?"

"Ummm, no."

"Jack, I'm a religious person. Told my husband, 'If we come home from Arizona and see Jack show up, it's a sign that's meant to be.' Coming home, we saw your stuff, then you! This is it! Got forms? How did you know?" Y was laughing so hard.

Of course I had no idea and no forms. But we got together next morning. And ended up setting a crazy record for them.

* * *

THANK YOU so much, J & Y! To 24/7 life by the river!

I can't read minds, but can read texts and emails. Call our local hotline at 909-262-3132 for a free reading of what the future might hold for your home value. Disclaimer: Operator standing by has no crystal ball, but has fortune cookies.

Always Take The Shot

Not basketball.

There are many more stories and moments I will never share. But they live in my heart, with many captured in pictures.

There's the couple celebrating their sixty-eighth anniversary. Or hugging someone who survived a scary accident. The tender cradling of someone's baby. Those poses with your pets! And young Jack, with his dog Cooper, and our goofy pictures. My selfie with E. How about the energetic 80-year-old on his roof? This book is just the tip of my memory iceberg.

Anything funny, special or beautiful.

Maybe it's just me, because I'm visual. My wife will attest to my washed out memory, except when there's a photo that helps me vividly relive the moment.

As I worked on this book, I laughed, lingered and sometimes teared up going through my Chino Hills album of over 4,000 images and some videos.

* * *

THANK YOU, my Chino Hills family and friends. You all have SO enriched my heart, nourished my soul.

We all have one shot at every moment.

For any picture, I always ask permission.

For life, we need to take every opportunity. It's all there waiting for us.

April 12

Laughing Lemonade

I've only visited with T over the years. But not his wife.

Until this day. As I walked away after leaving the latest update, the front door opens and I hear my name.

"Hi, Jack! I'm S, T's wife. I told T next time I catch you I'll introduce myself. T always told me you were a nice guy, not pushy or anything.

I read your book. It made me realize how hard you worked. But what got me was how uplifting it was, because you never know what others go through to be where they are, and how you were willing to openly share your difficulties, and even turn them into some really funny stories."

Yes, I was speechless. How could I not be?

S, THANK YOU so much for your kind words and gracious insights.

* * *

Turning lemons into lemonade. Have had lots of practice, after tons thrown my way. Some I even grew myself.

After a stinging early defeat, I remember telling John these knockdowns will NEVER go to waste. I'll look for a new lesson.

The bonus: How can I make my lemonade really tasty? My favorite challenge was to make it practical, witty and if possible, funny – whether it was the moment itself, or at least the way it can be presented.

You'll see it in the playful titles, many I've agonized over. Where I can be the ultimate butt of the punchline, I volunteer myself. Never had laughing gas, but I want to be the best laughing lemonade maker.

From that time, John has often said, "OK, Jack. Let's see how long it takes you to whip a funny story out of THAT!"

EVERY defeat is painful, costly and humiliating. Yet it'd be such a waste to hide them in the shadow of the negative, when we have paid the tuition in full, with no returns or refunds.

So - I hope you've been enjoying these sips, every page infused with its own unique flavors and ingredients.

Why go sour...

When we can go soar?

P.S. I know you've seen Jesus on a tortilla...but this?

April 12

Telltales Of A Tall Tale

"Everyone here knows you sold the house around the corner. Couple days ago two ladies were here, telling everyone *'THEY sold that home and had more buyers.'* Do you know them?"

G added, "I asked them if they knew you, and they said, 'No.' After I told them I knew you & John sold it, they quickly left."

And G wasn't the only one who thought something was not right, as I heard from several other neighbors.

While there were NO written claims they sold the home, by omission of required disclosures, it was the IMPRESSION they wanted to impart, despite not representing either side.

"Many cash buyers" is a stretch as they have NOT had a single buyer in more than 8 years.

While this involves multiple violations, it's nothing compared to 'big league' offenses you'll read about in this book.

Please keep an eye out. There are ALWAYS telltale signs.

* * *

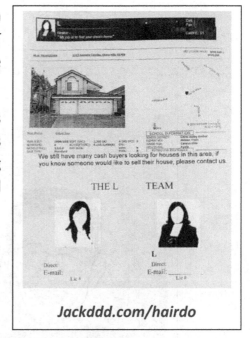

Jackddd.com/hairdo

Not our hairdos, but definitely our listing.

Backyard Eats

Wise guy: "What inspired the signs of the Western Zodiac?"

Jack: "Greek & Roman mythology, mostly."

Wise guy: "What inspired the signs of the Chinese Zodiac?"

Jack: "Why, the *menu*, of course!"

Wise guy: "Well, what about the Dragon?"

Jack: "You don't see any flapping around anymore, do you?"

(Confession: I concocted that joke above. 'Thank you,' or 'My apologies,' depending on your reaction.)

We've heard Chinese people ate everything with four legs, except the table. Lots of truth to that.

Did you know early 20th century American cuisine was just as adventurous? Imagine possum on fine china.

In an unexpected conversational detour, someone mentioned they don't waste what's perfectly edible.

"Like what?" I curiously asked.

"Oh, like squirrels, birds, snakes and rabbits in my backyard," as he shared preparations to best enjoy these delicacies.

I bet you never thought my joke would come true.

(At least he knows what he's eating. While I enjoy my hotdogs, McNuggets and Spam, no one really knows what's in them!)

April 14

Mull It Over

Or think about it. Just "hair" me out.

The first covid shutdown created an existential problem. While we're grateful real estate was an essential business, barber shops were closed down.

Knowing my hair grows about an inch every three weeks, at some point, the overgrowth might be enough to keep all of you safely and far away enough from me – imagine a spiky sago palm, just with black palm fronds stiffened with gel.

There was also the very distinct possibility of me showing up, sporting a - mullet.

My advance apologies. Although harmless, you will NOT be able to UNSEE this image.

* * *

You can grow yourself one at **faceinhole.com***.*

Jackddd.com/mullet

Ditched

X was always kind and funny. But through the years, I saw him grieve through the unexpected loss of his wife.

Years later, he shares happy news of meeting someone. But it wasn't meant to be, telling me when it ended, "She was nuts!"

While I never ask, he had said many times, "Jack, when the day comes, you know you'll be listing my home." I certainly appreciate it, and we never take it for granted.

"Guess what - I got engaged! And, uh, I'm sorry. I know you're the best agent, and friendliest, but my long time buddy who doesn't do much really wants my listing, so I gave it to him."

Looks like I was the one ditched at the listing altar...

His next door neighbor, someone I served in another career, also often reminded me I'd get his call if the day ever came.

His home hit the market, and he happened to be outside...

"Hey Jack, so sorry, buddy. It just happened so quickly. And I honestly totally forgot you!" he said with a warm smile.

* * *

In my worst moments, just the attempt to find the humor and wit is a life-saving jab into my system. My first thoughts made me laugh so hard, I had to wipe my stupid smile off before the next door. The original punchline was a gloriously vindictive pun. You just enjoyed the much kinder alternative ending.

April 20

Write On!

It's been exciting to meet fellow authors around town.

Erik Simonsen has published two books on military planes.

Dennis Muñoz titled his children's book, "Punky the Penguin's Special Day." I look like a senior citizen, but have a kid's heart.

I know someone famous in town who talks about cataloguing her dog rescue stories, one of these days.

Another lady has a book in her, about the little snapshots of life she's seen and overheard as a school crossing guard.

In a curious twist of opposites, someone penned a pint-sized but powerful piece on the love of God, while another gave strong arguments for dumping the organized church.

Diana Keuilian has two recipe books for cooking without all the bad stuff. REALLY want someone to pull no punches when you need a punch in your face? Just look up Bedros Keuilian.

X co-authored a women's devotional, and one for children*.

"Jack, looking forward to you selling our house someday!" she handwrote in ink on my autographed copy.

When they listed their home with someone else, I guess I got written right off the page. Or maybe she had writer's block.

*Amazon carries all books mentioned. (*It's beautifully illustrated for (grand)parents and younger ones to spend time and color together. Contact me for title if you're interested.)*

A Taste of Chino Hills

Once a week, my wife and I look forward to our fun date meal. A smiling "Hit the spot!" from my wife would be a success, as I try to avoid "I'll hit you on the spot!" blah restaurants.

I came across a brand new place, called "Lasa," the Filipino word for "taste." The featured dishes looked tantalizing enough to lick right off the page. But tucked in the write-up was a cryptic, "Chef Chad & Chase grew up in Chino Hills."

After a feast of unique flavors, I had to ask.

"Chase, hope you don't mind me asking. I visit around 10,000 families in Chino Hills. Curious where you guys grew up?"

"Man, it's been such a long time..." Although the street name escaped him, he knew HOW to get there.

They said their house was on the left, near the cul-de-sac, so I just named the neighbors one by one, until he said,

"That's it. They were to our left, and so-and-so to the right! How are they all doing? Can't believe how you just did that!"

With so many restaurants in LA, we almost never repeat. Lasa is one of a handful on our "can't wait to go back" list.

* * *

Chad & Chase, so nice to meat you. Wishing you all continued tasty success!

*Foodie? Don't miss out. LASA, 213-443-6163, **lasa-la.com***

April 23

DUI

I can always count on a warm greeting from J & M.

It was almost 6 PM on a beautiful early evening when their front door swings open.

"Hi Jack! How about a glass of wine?"

"Well," I said, "I don't think you want me getting a DUI. Might not be a pretty sight if I was staggering down the middle of your street, and get cited by Chino Hills' Finest, and have my mug shot splashed on the Champion, for

'Door knocking under the influence.'"

Up, Up and No Way

Superman always got the "away" part done nicely.

Not me.

C & K's cool motorhome has a small compartment in the back that could be a little garage for a tiny vehicle.

"You think my car would fit?" I curiously asked.

"Don't see why not," C said.

"Let's give it a shot. That would be funny," I said, tossing him my keys.

Here's a few seconds of actual video footage.

Listen for the crunch.

Ouch.

Oh well. It was worth a few chuckles to C & me.

Video at Jackddd.com/noway

April 26

---

*NOTE: Some light bathroom references, from the get-go. I was the one running for cover when someone else turned on the fan.

MAN, URE The Best Agent

"Hey, Jack, just listed my home with my buddy from (Another City). He really doesn't know much about Chino Hills, and since you're the best agent I know, can you – "

That little " – " (dash) is not tiny. We've been asked to: stop by and make further recommendations, pre-market, include and feature their home in our print, online & Asian mobile ads, fine-tune price points, and remember their home when I go around marketing OUR actual sellers' homes.

"Hi, XYZ, I really appreciate the kind words. Please understand we can't even legally do any of that without a contract. You're also asking me to perform services for free, services that our clients actually pay for. It's not fair to them, nor to us."

In one instance that went off the pasture, an individual decided to splat my name around their neighbors like a stinky poopsicle, citing my response out of context.

I'm grateful another couple confronted me. I simply showed them the question the individual asked me.

* * *

My wife bought the rather effective citrus-scented Poo-Pourri. Might preemptively spritz myself daily, in case anyone decides to go off, or go, on me.

"Jack, I'm Sorry. I Listed With My Friend."

In school, punctuation was just a bunch of squiggles my teachers made a big fuss over, an excuse to subtract a few points to deny me a perfect score. (Asian parents have been known to consider any score under 100 as abject failure.)

None of them told me it could also be the difference between much joy and sorrow in my business life.

I personally prefer getting the same sentence, but WITHOUT the '.' (period) after the word 'sorry.' *(Try reading both statements aloud, especially noting the punctuation.)*

"Jack, I'm sorry I listed with my friend." ☺

When C's neighbor first listed their home, I never even met them. C then tells me she already told them to call me, and gave me their number as well.

As is often the case, it was out of obligation that they listed with a relative, who lived in a different city, far, far and away.

Once the process began, they saw the many challenges that came with it, issues of distance, familiarity, marketing, responsiveness, feedback, service, etc. And frankly, results.

* * *

THANK YOU, J & Y, for allowing us to do our absolute best for you. Wishing you and your family many happy years ahead, as you leave us here in the IE, and upgraded to the OC!

April 27

Shello! Oyster Anybody Home?

Unlike the big, bad wolf, I've never pounded anyone's door down, or tried to mussel my way in.

But nothing is more exciting that walking up to a home that's been quiet as a tightly shut clam, and finally see it open.

"Well, Hello, Jack! We finally meet. I'm J. I'm N. So nice to meet you!" they both greeted warmly from their garage.

"We just get busy and never answer the door. But we know who you are, as do our neighbors. We always look forward to your newsletter. We can tell the effort and the quality of it."

Then J goes, "Wanna show you something. Come over here."

He pulls open a drawer, and in it are portions of my flyers that have been neatly cut, and stacked.

"After N reads it, if there's something important she feels we should know or do, she clips it, files it, and becomes part of MY honey-do list."

Aw shucks.

* * *

At a fancy restaurant, I remember our server saying, "Chef is really happy when we take back plates like yours. Not a lick left." To J & N, and every one of you who have honored me with your time reading through our "made-from-scratch" and "home-cooked" reports, THANK YOU SO MUCH!

Door Babe

Every now and then, after I got into real estate, my wife would mention something like,

"Do you know someone named N? She's really nice. Beautiful home too. Was there once for a party."

Of course, she never has a last name. Needle in a haystack.

Not this time. She knew the neighborhood, and remembered her husband's business.

Walking up to a home, I see a truck with that line of work.

The front door opens, and I'm greeted by a very gracious lady. And her name is N. And the home is nice, for sure.

Before I left, I had to ask.

"N, may I ask you something? Would you happen to know someone named Hedy? From Jazzercise years back? She was the 'door babe,' signing people in."

Her eyes lit up, smiled, and said, "Oh my God! No way! She's your wife? She was always one of the nicest people I knew for all those years. Please tell her I said 'Hello!'"

* * *

Over the years, the unexpected "Are you Hedy's husband?" or "Are you Jack's wife?" incidents continue to trickle in like a slow, delightful leak from a confidential file.

April 28

As Seen On TV

No, not those late night product infomercials.

As I walked up to their home, X, the wife, saw me.

Never really met her, but I can hear,

"Honey! Your friend's here!"

She sounded friendly enough, so I walk over to say "Hello" to Y, the husband, whom I've met before.

To my surprise, I get chewed up!

"I DON'T NEED THAT! GO AWAY!"

Now that's teamwork.

As I limp off to the next home, I thought, "Felt like I was on Animal Planet!"

* * *

We watched so many animal shows as a family. It's a familiar scene, as we all root for the young baby something fleeing for its life. Then things go into slow motion, and the poor critter gets shredded as my girls are screaming through the nine replays from different angles.

Fortunately, I only get 'eaten' at that house. Not unlike a video game, every next door gets me a reset and I'm alive again.

Life gives us so many chances. Dust yourself off, and try again. Never allow those who care for you the least affect you the most.

Oh, Great!

The supreme grill master of our home is m....y wife, of course. She's the one who has taken the best care of us, spoiling us with her home-cooked meals for over three decades.

On the menu was a bundle of asparagus.

As the flames kissed and made their marks of the spears of green, one decided to roll off deep into the bottom of the barbeque.

Between my corny ears and mind, I told her:

"Oh, GRATE!"

As always, the only thing that rolled were her eyes.

In happy OCD news, we all still got the same number of spears.

I guess the extra one was a -

SPARE-agus.

* * *

She's been subjected to things like that for forty years – she became my girlfriend back in 1981.

To her horror, none of our three daughters were spared of that gene, each of them infected to some degree.

To her credit, and our surprise, she usually coughs up one or two of her own a year.

May 1

WHACK-inito

Apparently some of you get a kick out of calling me by my entire, legal first name, Joaquinito.

I appreciate how smoothly it rolls off your tongues, leading with a secondary accent on the first syllable, emphatically dragging out the third syllable, dropping off into the fourth. 'HWA-kee-**NEE**-to.'

Properly pronounced, it always sounds the same.

Whenever anyone asks how to say it, I simply cannot resist having you give it a try.

Somehow, it's a magical moment when my name gets butchered, as new and unexpected sounds and syllables are spontaneously spit out, with a chuckle or two.

Don't remember how we got on to the topic of my real name, but somehow they were up for it. Taking turns giving it their best, one of them blurts out a gem worth me waiting fifty years for. Can't believe we got it on video!

* * *

THANK YOU so much Xander, Cayden & Mom for the laughs.

Jackddd.com/name

Stand-Up

"You mean, as opposed to me just sitting down and telling these stories?"

Never thought of myself as funny. Punny maybe, as my wife and daughters have been pummeled by my puns.

"Jack, we know you're not trying to be funny. But those stories you just told us, those are nuts. That's some funny stuff."

I get a lot of questions, and it's always great when I have an actual situation that answers it with accuracy and humor.

Never forgot the particularly painful but sidesplitting segment on TV, where celebrities were asked to read, on live camera, their own hate mail.

"Ooooh. Got those," I muttered to myself. It'd be such total ownage. It'd be hysterical for you, and a hysterectomy for me.

Can't believe some of you have seriously suggested I hold an event like this. If we did, I'd donate 100% of the proceeds back to our community. And every paying attendee gets to roast and embarrass me. Yikes.

But careful what you ask for. I've taken enough notes there's a good chance many of you in the audience will get your own "Ding Dong" moment.

TBA

May 4

Cracks In The Pool

At our open houses, it is not unusual for entire families to come through the front door.

Curiously, one household started their tour from the back yard, with a refreshing dip in the pool.

Although her kids enjoyed it, she never wrote an offer.

(FYI: Swimming pool issues often scare off potential buyers – from coping separation, non-working filters or heaters, replastering to cracks...)

For this particular executive home, we were happy there was nothing to disclose regarding any cracks in the pool.

Just a few little quacks.

Jackddd.com/duck

A Fan's Fan

It was a warm day when I saw M & J.

As we sat in their living room, J excused herself, and came back with a little black fan, no larger than the palm of my hand.

"You should get your wife one of these portable fans! It's the BEST thing I got for my hot flashes! I've had this for a while and it's still going strong. Let me show you its blowing power!"

Enthusiastically turning it on, I was blown away.

It was the closest thing to a pocket-sized hurricane-in-a-hand.

* * *

It was a week away from Mother's Day. Amazon Prime shipping allowed me to feel like a man's man, when I got my wife one, delivered with days to spare. It's been two years, and that little wind machine is still blasting away, and has served her well.

A fantastic value at about $20. Look for the Innobay Personal Fan. You can thank me later.

May 11

Zoom

Thanks to a pesky virus, not a bacterium
We've mostly been stuck inside some room
Some cleaning & sweeping all day with a broom
Don't let your hearts fill with doom or gloom

Sent to the garage, thanks to my loud volume
Two cars already there in my new boardroom
Smart guy, Eric Yuan who let his idea bloom
An app millions and millions use, called Zoom

Show your face if you remember to groom
Hide under a blanket if still in your bedroom
We're all safe from morning breath or perfume
Only leave if your house needs a termite fume

Virtual backgrounds are your room in costume
Why be boring? Cheer up your workroom!
How about a picture of you sitting in the bathroom?
Check out mine. Might make you go, "Hmmm."

When our normal lives can start and resume
A little red Jackmobile's ready to VROOM!!!

P.S. Got good news of a grandson in the womb
Found out on FaceTime...it's just like Zoom

* * *

Let's see if you can figure out my
"quirky" Zoom video background.

Video at Jackddd.com/zoom

Can You Be My Dad?

D & D are obviously awesome grandparents. I often see D playing with his grandson, spending the time with him.

His grandson is super-smart. He even spelled "catastrophe" in one go for me, and made sure I knew what it meant.

Wise for his years, what he said once caught us unprepared:

"Grandpa, can you be my dad?"

I don't recall what D said, but I thought to myself, "For him to frame such a question, he must first have a concept of what a father is, and should be, and separately, who a grandpa is. Then he entertains the possibility and asks. What must be happening in his young world to take his mind and heart that way?"

Talk about deep (& scary) wisdom out of the mouths of babes.

Oh, by the way, our little philosopher is only TWO years old.

* * *

Although our three daughters are grown, I'll always be their dad, and they'll always be my girls. As they lead their own lives, we're separated by time and distance and just life.

I know I've failed in ways big and small while trying to be the best dad to them. But I also know I'll continue to strive to become someone my daughters would always want to be their dad.

May 16

DOoRK nocking

Knock, knock, knock!

"Who is it?" says the voice behind the front door.

"Hi R, it's only me, Jack. How are you?"

"Jack? Jack who?" answers R, still behind her closed door.

"Jack, um, real estate, funny-looking agent, Jack?"

"Oh, you mean, Ding Dong?"

"Yes, that too."

"Oh why didn't you say so," as the door finally opens and I'm greeted with a smile.

*

"Please knock loudly!"

It's usually handwritten, precariously taped close to the door.

Now that's my kind of sign - the dreamy opposite of a "No Soliciting" notice come true.

Not really. Their doorbell's just broken.

* * *

That's NOT the only time I've been remembered as Ding Dong. If the DMV ever allows personalizing with an eighth letter, my KNOK NOK plate will become DING DONG.

I'm happy to answer to that name. I've answered to worse.

Look Ma, No Hands!

In one iconic poster, Marilyn Monroe is in a white dress when she suddenly meets a gust of wind.

At least she has hands.

This is what happens when you only have ribs...

Surprisingly, there were no feelings of embarrassment. But there was some serious damage.

Jackddd.com/ribs

May 17

Miracle On A Chino Hills Street

We were all praying, hoping and working hard for one.

"In 25 days, the family we love dearly across the street are going to be without a home. It's either a private loan, or an investor who'd be willing to buy it and keep them as tenants. We just know you're the guy for this," Lynda shared.

At 29, J had a spinal cord tumor. The surgery was a success, but he went numb from above his stomach to his feet. He's disabled, eligible for subsidies, yet works daily, driving a vehicle equipped with hand controls.

Their kind landlord who charged them a low rent for ten years had just passed away, and his heirs wanted it sold.

Before we were informed the sellers had no intention of paying any commissions, John & I already decided we were going to give it everything we got. Videos were posted to social media, my site and their story was provided to both local and Chinese real estate publications.

And then, I went door-to-door to share their story.

Four days and 281 doors later, T tells me, "OK, Jack, I'll talk to my wife when she gets home."

Next day my phone rings in the car around noon. "After I read their story and watched the videos, I couldn't stop thinking of that family. Can we see the house and meet them?"

Had to pull over. Really hard to drive with hopeful happy tears.

That first meeting was touching, as the Knicks' kids gave T & C smiles & hugs, an instant tender connection between them.

As we left, T & C instructed me, "Jack, STOP telling anyone else about this. **This family is ours.**" Despite every bump, when they had good reason to back out, THEY reminded us, "The main reason we are doing this is to help this beautiful family."

There are many to thank: The old landlord and his family; Marianne at the Champion; Lynda, who tirelessly did so much for the Knicks; and the many friends, neighbors and church family coming with prayer, love and support, time and again.

We are SO happy for J, N & their three beautiful kids - having gone through so much, yet through trials and uncertainty they have only shown a spirit of COMPLETE joy and trust in God.

Our buyers added: "We're blessed to have an opportunity to help the Knicks. Who knew? Felt like it was a 'meant to be' situation waiting to happen. Thanks for knocking on our door that day. **Oh, now we know WHY all those other investment properties over the years somehow NEVER panned out.**"

T & C's kids won't have to look past their own Mom & Dad for an example of incredible love & generosity.

* * *

THANK YOU. What a privilege for John & me to be a part of this Chino Hills miracle!

(Has anyone invented wipers for my eyeballs yet?)

May 18

A Little Something Something

Over years visiting this one street, the corner house was still a mystery. Until this one afternoon.

A black SUV is on the driveway. With nothing to lose, I hang a U-turn, and park my car across the street and hop out.

"Oh, you're the real estate guy, right? On my way out. But we are selling. Call me in two hours."

Next morning at 10, we get together and sign the listing. As we sat there, E looks at me, then at my partner John, and asks:

"Hey Jack, can I ask YOU something?"

We all look at each other, and he continued:

"Hey Jack, are you **ON** something?"

We start laughing, as John told him I didn't even smoke. E asked why I looked genuinely happy anytime he's seen me.

I said, "You're looking at the most grateful goofball running around town. I'm met with kindness. I've never really met you, and you greet me saying you know me, and are selling with us. We don't take that for granted, and are just thankful for so many families like yours. How can I NOT have a smile?"

* * *

It's not that we don't have any problems in business or life. We have them. Lots. But what we can fix, we fix now. What we can't, we just let it go. For everything else, I'm grateful.

2004: The Prequel

As a soon-to-be new agent, I attended many training seminars. At this one in Riverside, it was jammed. Looking for an open seat, I thought I spotted a familiar face.

"Hi, is that you, Debbie? Do you remember me?"

*

In 2004, long before I was in real estate, I thought of selling everything to be debt-free. As a close friend owned a brokerage, he said he'd send us his best Chino Hills agent.

When Debbie came, she said, "Since you and our broker are very close friends, instead of the usual 6%, we're reducing it to only 5%. Sound good?" Everything was signed in minutes.

That night, I told my wife, "Are you OK if I call them tomorrow and redo the contract? I did the math. I am expecting her, his best agent, to do the best work for us, but she just got her gross commission shrunk by 33%, before she even gets her share. You know I work hard, and I don't think that's fair to her." She agreed.

*

She looked up, and after a few moments, said, "Jack! I do remember you! Of course I do. How do you forget the only seller who rips up the discounted commission contract, and tells you to rewrite it at full commission? I never forgot that!"

We ended up NOT selling, but that's a whole 'nother story.

May 21

Shirt Happens

After we had a chance to catch up, D gets up, says he has 'something' to show me. He was at a thrift store when something caught his eye. "Cool design," he thought. Looking closer, he goes, "Oh wow. I HAVE to buy this."

I've never been so vulnerable and unprepared, as he unfurled a brown shirt. My tears started falling. Just couldn't stop.

Before real estate, one of many businesses I attempted and failed in was t-shirt designing. A year-long artistic adventure, it ended badly, scarring me financially, and more deeply, artistically – because every design was a little part of me. I only sold two, and fortuitously one of them ended at the thrift.

That shirt brought back all the memories, shame, pain and regrets of my four darkest years, as I attempted over a dozen businesses that failed, struggling to provide for my family.

"I couldn't believe seeing your name on the copyright, and had been waiting for you to stop by and surprise you," said D.

Smiling, D adds, "And how God has mightily blessed you, Jack," holding up my latest flyer, pointing to the full page of listings. Never found the 'pause' button for my tears, but these new ones had smileys on them.

* * *

THANK YOU, D. *You have no idea just how deeply God used you, in one moment, to touch and heal my heart almost ten years later.*

Jackddd.com/shirt

(I designed this snowflake to spell out the Greek word, "tetelestai," which means, "It is finished" – Jesus' last words on the cross. The lower case letters start at the 12 o'clock mark going clockwise.)

May 22

When A Picture Is Worth A Few Words

As S & I were visiting, he gets a text from his wife, M.

He takes one look, and starts laughing.

"Wanna see what she sent me?" he asked.

"Sure!" I said, curious whatever it was.

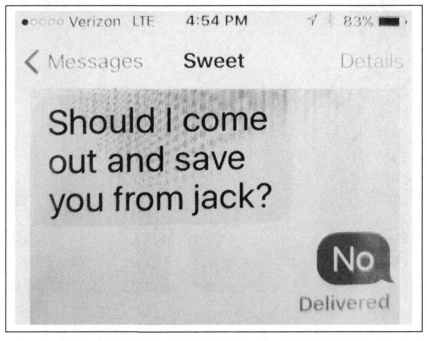

* * *

S & M, THANK YOU for making me laugh my head off. You both know how much I appreciate you and always have a blast dropping by.

Don't Like Jack? You're Still Covered

John & I are grateful for the support from thousands of you. Because Chino Hills is where we live and work, this is where we wanted to give back in a meaningful way no one was doing.

With apologies to the many worthwhile causes, instead of giving a little here, a bit there, we decided to do ONE thing, and hopefully make a real difference.

After chatting with a family who wanted a Ring doorbell, but didn't have the funds at that moment, the lightbulb went off.

SO, if you're a Chino Hills homeowner in areas we actively serve, and are 70 years old or better (was 80 and up in 2018), and don't have a video doorbell, we provide you one for FREE.

You also get one if you're a homeowner under 70 who has any physical disabilities; or one of you actively serves our armed forces away from home; or you are a widow.

Baked into our disclaimers was you "never have to be a client, past, present or future." And though funny to many, I was serious when I added, "You DON'T even have to like Jack."

That moment finally came when I had to reassure one family that despite being on someone's "unlike" list, we were honored to provide them one. That "Jack clause" was there from the start, and I meant it. Simple as that.

(As of 12/31/2020, we've provided over 375 free doorbells. Most updated project details at 91709jack.com/safe.)

June 3

Safe Se.....

(John & I have taken precautions to be as careful as possible in working through the covid times to keep all our sellers, buyers, and our own families safe.)

By email, by phone call or by text
A buyer or seller, with us connects
"How's the market?" one always asks
Wanting trusted help on what's next

Stay six feet apart, everyone checks
Mouths, noses and faces with masks
(Did any wish this virus be big as T-Rex
Instead of being tiny gross liquid specks?)

Buyers viewed virtual tours and pics
Inside and out, like floors and decks
Appraisers measuring, recording facts
Inspectors hunting, for dead wood and insects

New forms, new rules, some complex
The new mobile notary is really FedEx
With DocuSign, you just sign and affix
With Zoom, see faces with a few clicks

Balsz is German, but John says mostly Mex
The golf course is his favorite way to relax
Jack is Chinese, but born ugly - was it a hex?
(FYI as a child he could spell Archaeopteryx)

John & Jack never use short term gimmicks
Just marketing, service and results to the max
Even since covid, new sellers into their mix
New buyers & escrows as each side interacts

Time seems slow, as the second hand ticks
While many baked or binged on Netflix
John & Jack been busy practicing safe selling
Goodness gracious, what were you thinking?

P.S. Too close, we can be at each others' necks
Hope no partner will soon be each other's ex
When it's your spouse always ignore all defects
Say "Yes," "I'm sorry" & hand them your checks!

* * *

Many of the lines and ideas were formed in one sitting right after I woke up, with no rush to get ready to go anywhere. (Or more like one staring, as I lay flat on my back, fixated on the blank ceiling to concentrate.)

This version has been further revised from the original.

June 5

Buffed By The Scratch Slayer

J just returned from a trip to the mountains, and was showing me how the sides of his giant truck got all scratched up.

"Well, funny you mention that. Just got some crazy scratches from a detailing job gone bad. We were selling our daughter's Corolla, so I told them to wax the WHITE car. My car isn't very white. It's RED. But they started to work on it."

"Hmmm, let me see. Bring your car over here," said J, as my car was parked close to his home that day for my visits.

He tried some product, but nothing happened.

"Hey, J, no worries. You don't have to do that. Thank you!"

Later, on the way back to my car, I see him waving me over.

"Check it out. What do you think?" said J, with his serious but big smile.

Whoa! I could NOT find the scratches.

THAT was so kind of J. I don't think it came off in a few buffs.

* * *

J, THANK YOU so much. While I'm totally surprised by what you did, I'm NOT surprised you would do something like that. You & P have always been the kindest to me.

The Jackmobile is grateful too. He thinks beauty is only a coat of paint deep. Now my shallow brat wants a real detail.

Remote (Out Of) Control

Setting up the Jackbrella is about a three-minute sidewalk side show. Or freak show.

As I started, a couple across the street was definitely wondering what I was doing.

"You're more than welcome to watch me put it all together, if you have a few minutes for a quick laugh," I said, inviting them over.

"It has a remote control? Can you show us how it works?" asked E.

I've never really played with the remote. Today was as good a day as any. Why not?

Video at Jackddd.com/remote

And while I'm at it, let's see if I can make it – oops!

(Just watch the crazy video. For best results, turn UP your volume.)

* * *

A very special THANK YOU to F & E for recording my reckless remote uncontrolled moment. So nice to meet you both!

June 6

Do They Like You?

6:46 PM, getting dark fast. It's time to head home. Usually.

"Whatever you do, please go next door NOW. Do they LIKE you?" C asked.

"They're pretty nice to me. I sure hope so," I responded.

"I *think* they're thinking of selling, But you didn't hear that from me!" whispered C.

Their front door opens, and F greets me with, "Oh, Hi, Jack! Great timing! Honey, Jack's here! Come on in!"

After the sign went up, another neighbor, J, flagged me down.

"You know, C was mad. She thought you didn't end up with the listing. Had to explain and reassure her that the "John & Michelle" sign IS John & Jack."

*

On a rainy day, a packed sanctuary gathered to pay our respects to C, who was at once intelligent, kind and funny.

As the service concluded, her dearest friend A asked if I could stay for one more thing. Of course. And as only C would do, we got to visit with one another while building our own ice cream sundaes, loaded with all the fixins.

C, to say I'll miss you would be so inadequate. You finished your race perfectly in His time, but too soon for us. THANK YOU always for your kindness and joyful ways.

Gulper Eel

I've been handed all sorts of liquids – from bottled water, iced water, sodas, homemade juices, even a fancy lemon granita.

Sipping to quench my thirst, it took everything NOT to drop my jaw and spray everything out, with what I heard:

As they took out another water bottle, they casually mentioned,

"We always reuse and refill our own bottled water. Why pay more, right? Here...want some more?"

What would YOU do?

Growing up chugging puke-inducing (but effective) Chinese herbal broths, I had the training to "Keep Calm, and Glug On."

None of this "I didn't inhale."

I didn't just inhale.

I imbibed.

* * *

From childhood I've always been fascinated by the weird and unusual in the animal kingdom, especially those from the depths of the sea.

The gulper eel is a favorite, perhaps because it's dark-skinned with a rather big mouth. Like me. Google it.

*On this day, though, I felt like I was **gulping eew.***

June 15

We Will Take It Sitting Down

Over the years, John & I continually improve our presentation to meet your needs. It is, in my humble opinion an ongoing work of living art, solidly framed by cold hard facts and figures, aggressive and effective marketing, and indisputable results.

When all goes well, we always come prepared. And though we are never the overbearing types, many times our sellers do want to get it all signed and going on the spot.

We were told up front P & C had already interviewed two other agents, even providing us their names. Thankfully, because what we do is so different from most, it doesn't change our presentation. It did allow us to provide third-party public information regarding their claimed 'big' production.

As we rested our case, C broke out with a smile, and also broke into a rather boisterous round of applause for John & me.

"Bravo! The other two weren't even close! Honey, I'm ready to sign if you are," said C.

"I've been ready two YEARS ago!" P mumbled with a laugh.

C wasn't standing for her ovation, but some things in life we're happy to take it sitting down.

* * *

THANK YOU, P & C! So glad we could help you leave SoCal with a big smile, and big check. Clap! Clap! Clap! Clap!

June 18

House Divided

The only thing I play is a nylon string guitar.

I can still competitively swim on a mahjong table like an addicted gamer for hours.

While sports are so out of my radar, there are tidbits I've accidentally ingested, thanks to seeing it so many times.

What must it be like, sharing the same roof, double-dipping into each other's sauces, and yet disagree on things like:

USC vs UCLA

(First time I saw those pennants, I thought, 'How nice. They love them both!')

Then there are homes where I AM the thorn. One spouse welcomes me, while the other warns, "DO NOT COME BACK."

Of course, their marriage is way more important than me, so I avoid such homes altogether.

P.S. Got lucky once. During the few seconds skipping past their driveway, the friendly half comes out, and says, "Hi!"

* * *

FYI, here are a few videos I've recorded over the years. You can thank God there's no singing. Just fingerpicking. Not my nose. The guitar.
Jackddd.com/guitar

June 18

Mommy, Can I Take A Picture With Jack...

I appreciate the kind references to being one, from being well-known, at least in a few corners of our city, to having one-name recognition status.

There are the many sightings around town, although I feel more like a UFO. An 'Unexpected Flying Object,' with the word 'flying' to loosely mean 'the act of leaving a flyer.'

The true test of being a celebrity, is when someone asks to take a picture with you.

"Mommy, can I take a picture with Jack's 'thing'?"

Posing with her smile, the moment was captured.

* * *

THANK YOU, little girl! It made my day that the "thing" made you smile!

Other kids have decorated it with flowers.

Dogs mostly bark at it, a few have sniffed around it, and a discerning handful have seen it fit to baptize it with their bladders.

Jackddd.com/picture

Ready Or Not, Hair I Come!

Met Cooper long before I met his human family. He'd hang his paws on the wrought iron fence that kept him in, and I got to pet him because he was so friendly.

First time I met T, Cooper came charging past the front door and excitedly slammed into my legs!

T said, "I can see Cooper likes you, but he also just left all his hair all over your pants! Let me get the vacuum!"

No worries at all. As a well-loved page wears a dog ear, my pants & I show off dog hair as a badge of honor, hard work and above all, affection from my many four-legged buddies.

This was the last time I saw him, as we said goodbye to our wonderful clients S & T as they headed to their new home on top of a hill. Big hug from me, a few slurps from Cooper, and more hair. Miss you all!

Jackddd.com/cooper2

July 6

M Is For Magnificent

This is a GIGANTIC THANK YOU to someone very special.

Lots of planning go into the design and content of the newsletters and reports we've been providing all of you for years. We never do "fast food," canned or pre-packaged.

Like food, we're about local ingredients, diligently researched, and delivered "farm-to-table," almost as literally as the culinary term. We run our practice like a home-cooking grandma. We may not be related by blood, but we will always feed you (great information, that is) and treat you like family.

Can't even guess how much time M took to provide the incredible feedback on our neighborhood update. (You CAN enlarge the image to appreciate her detailed thoughtfulness.)

Within a few days almost all her suggestions were incorporated.

I must admit I almost fell of my chair for her to even say:

> *"Please don't take me off your list."*

TWICE.

* * *

M, are you kidding? THANK YOU for your super time and talent. You're simply Maggienificent!

Check out her detailed analysis and suggestions at:

Jackddd.com/improve

July 7

Robbert

"Hi Jack. My name is X. You don't know me, but you know my parents. It's time to think about selling their home. They've told me about you a few times, and can see they trust you, and always enjoy your visits. When can you stop by?"

We are keenly aware of the privilege and responsibility of receiving so many calls like that.

John & I get together with this one family to discuss such a situation. We present all the facts, our marketing & results, and answer their questions. They were in no hurry, and it would be months before any decision would be made.

The home is for sale that weekend, at our recommended price, with every description highlight based on what we told them made their home special, with an agent who had never sold a home in Chino Hills for many years, but was their friend.

John & I are big boys, and that's just part of our business.

But we felt like we got robbed. By Rob, of course. We didn't know we walked right into a bobby trap.

* * *

(Disclaimer: Aside from being such a common name, this Robert lives FAR away from Chino Hills, so it was safe enough to use to turn pain into pun. Looking back, he took a ton of notes. Another family who did this to us has a PERFECT last name. Unfortunately, it's "unusual," so I'll never say.)

July 12

No Soliciting, Part 2

An alternative title could very well be,

The Most Literal Dose Of My Own Medicine

(In one of my newsletters, I included a picture from the story, "No Soliciting, Part 1," which takes place almost a year EARLIER, which you'll be reading soon.)

Visiting H's door, I couldn't believe what was waiting for me.

She snipped out a portion of the picture from THAT very same flyer, and taped it to her front door.

That was really funny!

* * *

Great job, H! ☺

Happiness Is...

A "No Soliciting" sign mounted INSIDE the house, and practically covered by the vertical window blinds!

* * *

D & S, THANK YOU always for being so kind to me!

July 15

Commission

After opening escrow, John & I join our buyers at their soon-to-be home, who were relaxing with the sellers, like longtime friends.

Days later, we get disappointing news they decided not to sell, which they have every right to. It's part of life and real estate.

Until John calls me, and drops this gem:

"Hey, the sellers called our buyers directly. They're willing to sell to them on one condition: cut us out of getting paid..."

"...AND they want us, and our broker, to sign in writing, we would never sue them for the rightfully earned commission."

John & I have always committed to putting you, our clients first, no matter what, even in difficult situations.

All we needed to know was this was THE home for our buyers. They said, "Yes," and we agreed to take the short end of the stick. Wait – make that NO stick. First time we got an

omission check.

BONUS: Neighbor: "Jack! I'm so sorry you got ripped off!"

Apparently X wanted to make sure his savvy move did not go unnoticed, so he bragged about it to the neighbors.

* * *

Too bad. So much beautiful Bible stuff covered their home. And cars. Yet sometimes, such things just miss our hearts by inches.

A Taste Of Retirement

John & I made a pact to stick around for at least the next 15 to 20 years, health and mental capacities intact, God-willing.

He LOVES golf, but can't play seven days a week. My wife might go nuts. We both need something to do, anyways.

One time, I found myself taking a normal stride with my left foot, then gingerly drag my right foot up.

As familiar people drove past me, windows would roll down inquisitively.

"Hey Jack, you doing some Chinese exercise?"

"Well, not really. A little bit of my big toe nail got snagged in my sock last night, and I thought it'd be a great idea to yank out the little hanging bit."

Felt nothing much before bed. Woke up to "toetal" pain.

My plan to sit the day out was ended prematurely by boredom.

As I hobbled along at less than half my normal speed, it hit me:

"So THIS is retirement speed. Not bad at all."

Less that throbbing toe, please.

July 16

The Fuel Shack

The Green Machine Matcha Latte is not good. It's heavenly! Their plates and smiles are worth your drive to San Clemente.

After a knock on the door, Yolanda, and often Dave, would welcome me with giant smiles.

Once she found out I enjoyed food of almost every kind, I either got fed an incredible snack, or got to bring home a tasty morsel for later. There was homemade jerk chicken, banana bread in a bottle, and even avocado ice cream. Jealous yet?

The day came to make her dream of opening her own place a reality, and for Dave to suffer next to the surf. It was time to say goodbye. I felt happy and sad. Truly sweet and sour.

While many of you occupy permanent spots in my heart, it was only appropriate that I renamed a section of my gut to "The Quam Expressway."

Yolanda also taught me the "proper" way to hug. Left shoulder to left shoulder, heart meets heart.

Dave & Yolanda, you always treated me like a beautiful ham, generously sprinkled with tons of love, kindness, laughter and grace over time. THANK YOU from the bottoms of my heart and tummy. Special doesn't even begin to describe the both of you. **thefuelshack.com**

Jackddd.com/ fuelshack

What's In Your Garage? #2

There's a reason for everything.

"Just wondering why there are three really nice cars gathering dust on the driveway, baking under the sun?"

I'd usually be shown into the garage, where an even more exotic beast on four wheels is parked sideways.

Or, there's a mini-perfume factory in there.

Or, several bedrooms that shouldn't even be there.

I'm no automobile expert, but I appreciate fine art that can take me places and sound like rolling thunder.

When I finally met A & V, I asked the same question, seeing two late-model top-of-the-line German 4-door missiles that were both among my favorites.

"A, if these two gorgeous cars are out here, what on Earth do you have hiding inside your garage?"

"Nothing much, Jack. Junk. Just lots of junk."

Garbage* in the garage.

(*gar-BAZH please, if you'll indulge me for the rhyme.)

* * *

The original, but unrelated "What's In Your Garage?" episode is in Ding Dong #1, dated February 4.

July 22

Prays Together, Stays Together

There are doors that scare me.

With reasonable intelligence and the strong urge for self-preservation, I AVOID them.

One of our office managers once remarked, "Jack, you have the nicest clients!"

"I know why. ONLY the nicest families talk to me. Frankly, most people are."

With no intention of visiting this one door, having been verbally sprayed on many years back, I'm surprised to see both of them on the driveway, washing their cars.

Not wanting to come off as a jerk, I gingerly say, "Hi!"

Without missing a beat, BOTH gave me a shout-out. (Not the friendly kind.)

"YOU GOT FIVE SECONDS TO GET OUTTA HERE!" Etc.

I guess, aside from praying,

> The Family That Yells "Go Away!" Together,
> Also Stays Together!

* * *

*(I've NEVER done a thing to them. The most was a knock, which they've never answered, and left a newsletter. And I've skipped their home a long time ago. **Just the same, my sincerest apologies.**)*

High Speed, No Ticket

We take our time. We love what we do. We enjoy answering all your questions. And we love visiting with you.

Our average listing appointment goes anywhere from an hour to two. My marathon went for almost four hours.

At 1:32 PM, R & P called, "We found our dream home!"

"Congratulations! When are you guys coming back?"

"Not for at least another week, Jack. How quickly can we start the process of getting our home on the market?" asked P.

"We can send the listing agreement over by DocuSign."

"Let's do it!"

It was 2 PM when we hung up. After getting all the details, John sent it off.

By 2:11 PM, John texted me, "It's signed, time to go to work!"

Less than 10 minutes? I had to ask how they did it so quickly...

"R's driving, and I just did everything on my phone, cruising along the freeway! Piece of cake."

(They weren't driving fast. Only the signing was.)

* * *

Congratulations R & P, and to your entire family, who all found a sweet spot close to one another! That's priceless!

July 24

Answer To Prayer, Or...

"Honey, you've met Jack..."

(Actually, no. It's my first time meeting her.)

"He's the only agent allowed in the house."

(When I first met D, he made it very clear, he wasn't selling, and wasn't going anywhere. Then he adds, "But if you ever have a real, and I mean, REAL, buyer who's interested AND qualified, let me know.")

Today was THAT day. When they asked how soon they'd be ready to come over, I said within 30 minutes.

"Jack, either this is an answer to prayer, or a cruel joke. Just a few nights ago, we were thinking it might be time to sell. But we were wondering if we can do it WITHOUT ever going on the market, AND get a fair price. And you show up out of the blue, and tell us you have a qualified buyer?"

We presented both parties with the same comps, allowing each to arrive at their own seller's price & buyer's offer. We opened escrow in a week, at a very fair price for both sides.

* * *

The whole process was a delicate dance of three dominoes that had to fall perfectly. A few times it looked precarious. We absolutely appreciate everyone's patience throughout the almost half a year's time it took to close everything. THANK YOU TO ALL OF YOU!

Chinnovation Hills

Our city is home to extremely successful entrepreneurs and high-powered executives. It's a privilege knowing many of you as gracious people who also wear shorts, PJs and no makeup.

My soft spot goes to the mom-and-pop shops, the home-based budding businesses, and even young lemonade stand owners under Grandma's watchful supervision.

On a Sunday afternoon, I ran into Nico, who was on their eighth detail job for the weekend. Their portable tent and equipment went nicely with their work ethic, skills and smiles. And he's only a sophomore! Way to go!

Lourdes decided to make gentle soaps for her mom, whose skin started itching from ongoing treatments. That's how her unique GGB soap and soaking products started.

With lots of lockdown time and an "I can do that" attitude, Jackie began crafting her colorful custom theme art foldable tables. It's impressive to see her **taking immediate action on her intentions**. That is a rare quality at any age.

To contact the above local businesses, and see others you can support, please scan the QR code or go to **Jackddd.com/local**.

If you're a Chino Hills resident, with a business serving Chino Hills families, WHOM I KNOW AND HAVE MET, please send your info to jack@91709jack.com if you'd like to be included at no cost. (Complete details at jackddd.com/local)

July 26

Petal Attraction

In the happy mix of being a geek and doing my best to listen to our buyers, we customize home searches to actually show you only what you actually want to consider.

While the 100% perfect home doesn't really exist, unless one's pockets are bottomless, this home we were showing our buyers pretty much checked all their major boxes.

Relevant criteria is a necessary starting point, but nothing is more crucial than a walkthrough. Ever checked properties promising on paper, only to leave in minutes?

Or - your gut confirming the feeling of, "THIS is home!" within moments, barely walking through the entrance?

T & D are excited for this property. It was hard to miss their smiles getting wider.

"Jack, it's a sign! This is it!" D came over and exclaimed.

She takes me over, pointing to a delicate flower.

"That's my favorite! Been trying to cultivate one for years at the other home, and failed every time. And it's blooming here, and there's THREE of them!"

* * *

Congratulations, T & D! What a journey as the escrow on your special home came to a close.

Without a Glenn in sight.

Man Of Steel

Many are surprised that real estate as a business, is a full-contact sport that cuts and bruises, despite spilling no blood. In some ways you need to be like Superman.

"I know you work hard and sell a lot of homes here. But the best part is even my kids like you, Jack!"

That was the listing call I received from B, whom I've NEVER met. It is true, over the many years, I would hand the latest flyer to one of their children.

Over the next few months, a few things got in the way, and the process had to be temporarily postponed.

Nothing prepared me to wake up one morning, to see their home on the market just a few months later.

It was with a veteran agent John & I both knew.

A Man Of Steal.

* * *

My girls said I looked like Vector, the geek in "Despicable Me." In a presentation to agents, I told them that's what they see when they look at me. But when I look in the mirror, I don't see Vector. I see...(and I flashed a gigantic image of) Wolverine, because I need to heal no matter how many times I get shot or stabbed. And because he's got those six claws sticking out of his hands. Muahahaha!

July 26

chilDREn

"Jack, wanna know what my husband said when one of our neighbors, who's an agent, asked for our listing?" said X.

"He literally exclaimed, 'NO!' Then added he already had someone in mind, and finally said, 'Our son just got licensed.'"

Usually, when anyone's children get licensed with the Department of Real Estate (DRE), that's where all agents, myself included, gracefully bow out. And we happily and perfectly understand.

But as we sat down, X & Y shared a little more.

"Our son will represent us on the purchase of our next home. But we wanted him to see what happens when an agent works so hard year after year, builds a relationship that becomes a friendship; earns trust, never pushes, yet never once asks for the business. We wanted to show him that we wanted to reward an agent like that. You are that example to our son."

My journey of many successes is a giant tree built on one humbling instance after another. And this moment found me without words, as they smiled and gave me a hug.

* * *

*From an always grateful heart, THANK YOU, X & Y. Wishing your son incredible success in his own real estate career, and the blessing of meeting a world of beautiful families, especially just like **YOURS**.*

Jurassic Jack

A decent-looking monster flick is a must-see for me. The Jurassic-themed sequels, or any Godzilla movie would send me scurrying to Harkins. Subconscious leftovers from wanting to be a paleontologist as a kid.

It was our family outing for the night, my wife, middle daughter and I. Apparently half the city had the same idea, and the theatre was a packed can of sardines.

Having ended up in the rows closest to the screen, I slinked down as low as possible, so my neck wouldn't hurt.

As the mindless preshow flashed on, I see a silhouette set against the big screen rise in front of me, turn around in the almost-dark room, say,

"Is that you, Jack?"

My wife and daughter look surprised. I looked surprised.

It's hard enough to remember faces when I can SEE you, but an outline in the dark?

"It's L & A!"

"Oh, Hi there! Yes, from ABC Street! How on earth did you see me in the dark?"

"We didn't. We recognized your voice, Jack. Anyways, enjoy the movie – we had to say hello! See you soon in our neighborhood!"

July 28

Fish Wish

When an opportunity to do something comes up in front of my nose, I consider it a dispatch from heaven to go do something about it.

Several times I've been jokingly referred to as a bartender who makes house calls. I bring no fortified spirits, only two ears that many have felt comfortable enough to pour into it what's on their minds, and hearts at the moment.

Q had been on her own for years. She's funny and strong, her pets keeping her company. Doting family checks in on her as well. In one of our many visits, she happened to say she missed visiting the aquarium.

For a mural my daughter did with her friends, a local aquarium paid them in admission tickets. She had a few left, and asked if I knew anyone who would enjoy it.

What kind of perfect timing was that?

Ran it by her family to make sure it was OK, as they had to make the time to be there as well.

I appreciate my daughter offering her tickets for Q, her son, and granddaughter to be able to spend a wonderful day together.

Just glad I took good notes, and had a tight connection at the "Meet-A-Fish Foundation."

Does Length Really Matter?

She said hers was long. Really long - because she had been licensed for decades.

"I've been around longer than Jack. Doesn't he have complaints against him? And besides, the Asian buyers aren't really buying much anymore."

We believe in sharing the many ways we can uniquely serve you. That said, we don't mind objective side-by-side comparisons. We're often told we're a black sheep sticking out in a sea of white ones, but in a good way.

We've never thrown the first punch. But we never back down.

I presented R & Y with her five-year sales record: Zero last two years, and a total of six single family homes in Chino Hills.

Like the Israelites who once met their enemies with musical instruments, that day I showed up with my "accordion.*"

As R laughed, he asked, "So how many do you have?"

Just mine alone were 144.

R goes, "Wow. You guys make other agents look bad! Oh well, she asked for it by kicking you first." It's not making others look bad. Our track record is the result of relentless hard work.

As in life, how long one HAS a license doesn't matter. It's what one DOES WITH the license that matters.

*We have to leave some things as a surprise... ☺

July 30

Color Me Wine

As L & M wandered by the local Hobby Lobby, they somehow ended up signing up for art classes. With all the time in the world, why not?

It wasn't long when their home would be the closest thing to walking into an artist's café tucked in Paris in the early 1900s. Music filled the air, with a glass or two of wine. They sat across each other on a long dinner table, with their own canvas and easel, tubes of color and brushes surrounding them.

The best part was seeing a couple who were perfectly content with each other. That's what 'happy' looks like.

They painted whatever came to mind, from still life, to animals, plants, landscapes, and more.

Then L shows me a portrait he drew of his father-in-law the day he retired.

Not only was he free as a bird. He painted him flipping one too!

* * *

L & M, wishing you both many happy sessions of wine and art. Just make sure you don't drink the paint, or stick your brush in your wine.

Tool Box

It wasn't that I lost the listing, but HOW I was told I lost it. I can still see his face, oozing with satisfaction, eyelids at half-mast, wrapped in a smug smile. His wife? Always kind. That's a nail gun married to a soft terry cloth.

Met a few pliers, who extract as much information, before inflicting the pain of listing with someone else.

A lot of you are like a saw. It means a lot to hear you say, "Hey, we saw you here, saw you there, and saw you the other day!"

We don't mind getting measured and metered, compared and contrasted. We appreciate the diligent tape measure types.

It'd be nice to never meet another hammer. Or screwdriver. Or sheet of sandpaper hoping to grind us to a stump!

To all who performed ridiculous feats hunting for my contact information, you are my flashlights. (Asking your neighbors in the daytime works too.)

Many of you did your research, looking past the front of other glossy brochures. After locating the truth that sometimes can be hard to find, you make the well-thought out decision to call John & me. Guess that would make you... a stud finder! ☺

Our clients remark how John is so even-keeled, no matter what waves slap our escrows. He's the level.

Me? A few think I'm a tool, but I'm usually just a little piece of tape that sticks around.

August 1

What Do You Think I'm Calling You For?

"Jack, right? I know who you are. You know a couple of our friends too. Listen, got no plans to sell for a few more years. You've seen how much we've invested into our home, and we'd love to enjoy it for a while. But we'll keep you in mind."

That's how B greeted me first time we met.

Out of the blue I get a call from him.

"Hi B! How may I help you?"

"Jack, what do YOU think I'm calling you for?" with almost a rhetorical laugh.

"What happened?" I asked.

"We got the best Christmas present coming up. Make that PRESENTS. Our daughter's expecting twins for Christmas!"

Now that's a great reason to make a move.

Even if it's just four MONTHS later!

* * *

B & J, so happy for you, and your family. THANK YOU so much for letting us set a record for you, and for the multiple families you've personally recommended us to.

Enjoy your grandbabies, because they tend to grow too fast.

Keep Going

You'd be hard-pressed to find two more encouraging words, whether we are cheering on a toddler about to take her second step, or in the stands in the final seconds of a 100-meter dash. Or a setback that sets you on your back, and someone gives you a loving kick to set you right back up.

We've all said it. And hopefully heard it when we needed it.

Nothing saddens me more than budding relationships withering without warning. One did, after just two visits. Nice to ice.

Z came home, and seemingly waited for me. Despite scooting around to be as far as possible from their yard...

"NO ONE NEEDS YOU HERE...KEEP GOING! KEEP GOING! NO ONE NEEDS YOU HERE! NEXT DOOR DOESN'T NEED YOU, EITHER! THEY'RE NOT SELLING! KEEP GOING! GO! GO!"

I've been told to "Hit the road, Jack." But never with a supersized extra order of 'hit.'

Next door? They're pretty nice to me.

These instances are unavoidable. They're few and far between, but I truly feel bad, and sad, over every one of them.

But I'll always keep going. The inspired, relentless, always-looking-for-the-good-in-all-things kind of 'keep going.'

We all should.

August 5

Art Attack

During the covid lockdown, I got calls, texts and emails checking on me. I've never felt more loved as a neighborhood pest. That's like leaving a big piece of cheese for your favorite mouse, with a note saying you miss him.

(FYI: Thank you, E, for the 'Least Irritating Agent' title!)

And cards. Who knew Hallmark was still alive?

Some handwritten notes and letters.

And this hand-drawn card.

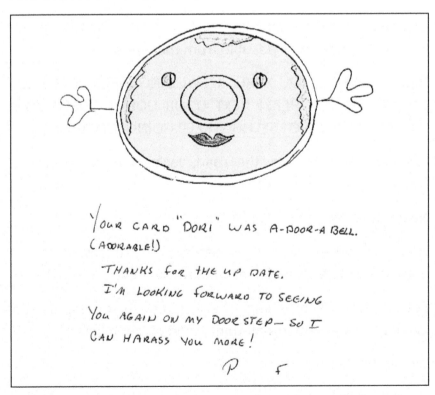

YOUR CARD "DORI" WAS A-DOOR-A BELL.
(ADORABLE!)

THANKS FOR THE UP DATE.
I'M LOOKING FORWARD TO SEEING
YOU AGAIN ON MY DOOR STEP — SO I
CAN HARASS YOU MORE!

P F

Who needs vitamins and vaccines when I have all of you?

Hitch The Road, Jack

There are times at day's end where I'm at the worst possible spot: at the top of some hill, while my car is at the bottom of the hill. And sunlight waning fast.

My usual solution is to go back to the last door, and literally ask them if they'd be willing to give me ride to my car. Thankfully, I've yet to be turned down.

On occasion, nobody would be home within a stone's throw. Stuck on the top of Rancho Hills (2.1 miles, longest street in Chino Hills, at least 282 homes on it), getting darker, I decided to throw my thumb in the air as I made my way down.

M came to my rescue, with the only caveat that I wouldn't sue him if we don't make it to my car, as his teenage son who just got his permit was on the wheel of their truck.

Another time, another M, whom I haven't met at that time, was my classiest lift. He rolled down his window, and said,

"Is that your little red car with "Jack" on it?"

Nothing like being cossetted by the fragrant supple leather of a luxurious S-Class, even for just a few minutes. And I wasn't even driving.

* * *

To each of you who have literally picked me up when I needed it the most, I APPRECIATE YOU!

August 7

Girlfriend

At some point almost everyone has a girlfriend.

"But SHE is really special," said K.

As she invites me in there's their adorable beagle to greet us. His name is Smeagol.

"Be right back, I want you to meet HIS girlfriend!"

Of course I'd love to meet a girl beagle. Beagless?

K goes into the other room, and comes back with his *precious*. Without missing a beat, Smeagol hops right up to the couch, and sits picture-perfectly right next to her!

Jackddd.com/girlfriend

August 8

Reactor Scale

It was my unusual idea of saying "Thank You"* to thousands of you who have put up with me for years. Making my rounds around town, each was personally signed, increasing each book's value by maybe a penny.

As soon as K saw me at her front door, she let out a loud happy scream! Ran back inside, zoomed back outside, and said:

"Oh my God! I've been waiting for you to stop by! SOOOO EXCITED for your book! Here's my camera! Let's take a picture! No, YOU TOO! Can you do a selfie?"

She zips back in her house, and comes back with a donation**.

At another home, R took the book, and blessed me with a SCREAM.

* * *

Thank you, K & R. You both registered a heart-shaking 10.0 on the Reactor Scale!

*How the first Ding Dong Diaries came to be was covered in the original book, May 3 page, "You Should Write A Book," and on pages 8 & 9, "A Very Special Thank You."

**My Ding Dong books were and will always be a gift from me to all of you. Except along the way a bunch of Chino Hills families did something magical. Continue reading, and you'll see. Can't wait? Flip to page 216, the December 31 story, "It's HER Fault."*

August 10

Special Security Clearance

Walking up, I found A enjoying the company of friends by the side gate of her house, nicely shaded on a hot day.

As I greeted her, I apologized for interrupting, and was about to head off.

Her friend goes, "Hey Jack, you can stay."

My senior brain goes into spasms when someone's face doesn't trigger the slightest clue.

"You might not remember me, but I live on EFG Street."

And with that, I remember his name, H, and his last name too, as it was pretty unique. While it didn't help that I've only met him once in all these years, it's not too hard when it's the only house with a giant wrap-around gate that keeps everyone and everything out except bunnies and snails.

As he introduced his wife, A, we all enjoyed some time together. Before we said our goodbyes, H says,

"OK Jack, the next time you come over, come on in. Here's how you get into my front door area."

* * *

THANK YOU, H, for the clearance upgrade!

Of course, your secret's safe with me.

August 12

No Soliciting, Part 1

(Our text exchange is reproduced in its unedited entirety.)

M: Jack, thank you for the book. I'm half way through and it is hilarious and a delight.

Jack: Hey thank you so much. Glad you're having a blast. Means a lot to have you guys say that.

M: Keep hustling Jack. You will be our first call when we decide to sell.

M: Oh and I added to my no soliciting sign

Jack: Oh wow. You guys just made my day. I laughed pretty hard for a second, but then it made me cry. Happy tears of course. Speechless right now. very humbled. Wow.

M: Glad it made you laugh. Your work ethic is truly inspiring and your comments in your book made me think about certain setbacks in my career. So it was more than a fun read it was helpful.

* * *

M & K and family, THANK YOU so much. Still speechless.

August 14

Dud Meets Spud

"So we're not in the book. How do we get in the next one?"

With that, B & S warned me to better watch out, because they would plan something. With a smile of course.

On another visit, as they unload groceries, an unfamiliar box caught my eye. What I thought was cereal was boxed potatoes. It said "Hungry Jack," so I posed with the box.

About a year later...

"We got something for you before you go," said B & S.

"Took a while, because I had to find a picture frame that had the right proportion," explained B.

I laughed and cried as I gently pried the back cardboard off, so they could autograph their very special gift to me.

jackddd.com/hungry

THANK YOU SO MUCH, B, S & C! Never mind the book. You got in my heart.

Are You FELINE The Love?

As I'm leaning on their couch, S goes,

"Don't move! Gimme your camera!"

One of their cats, Mosby, hopped up and decided to sit behind me. Then he moves closer. We look at the camera together. He stares at me. Before I knew it, he gently leans on my shoulder. I feel his soft and gentle nudge.

Then he squishes his head on my chest.

Other cats come up to me to rub off whatever was on them.

With Mosby, it was just a lot of soft, sweet, furry love.

Or was it because I smell like his litter? We'll never know.

More cute pics at Jackddd.com/mosby

In my catalog of adventures, Mosby is in a category of his own that will always live in my heart. Sadly, he has since passed on to the great cathedral in the sky. Will miss him so.

THANK YOU, B, S & C. Always love seeing you all, and so grateful you snapped that priceless moment with Mosby.

August 17

do

My dear Chino Hills families, you've given me the opportunity and privilege to achieve the ridiculous. The moderators who have invited me as a round table speaker seem to think so.

I have no fancy mantras.

You all know I don't even have a script, because I've NEVER asked any one of you for your business.

Serve you? Yes. Respect you? Yes.

Have a blast building relationships with all of you, year after year? That is the biggest blessing I have.

But I have to tell them something.

That's why those two little letters are in RED on the cover.

When I first gave K my book, he pointed right at it, and knew why it was there.

Actually, it doesn't just apply to real estate. Works pretty well with life.

DO something.

DO even just ONE thing.

If it works, DO it again.

If it doesn't, well, DO something else.

Repeat!

PALitics

That's what you get when politics is thrown into the mix of a friendship.

In many ways, I'm an observer of human nature, at its worst, at its best, and certainly everything in between.

"Can you believe who my friend ABC is voting for? How dumb can you get? I can't even believe it."

XYZ wasn't done yet.

"But no matter what ABC does, she will always be my best friend, because I love her."

Now that's worth fighting for.

The friendship.

Not the politics.

August 18

Top Secret Santa

Another day, another one of our many referred clients leaves a message they're ready to move, and how his wife had already headed over to their new home.

Since I've never met M, I asked how he came to call me.

"Told my brother we were selling. My company was going to have several relocation agents contact me. My brother stopped by the other day, and handed me your flyer, and said:

'Don't bother calling those other ones. THIS is the guy you want. Check out their marketing and the homes they sell. Just call him.'"

"Thank you so much! Who's your brother?" I asked.

My brian was still blank, even though I'm normally pretty good with names. He couldn't remember his brother's street, but described how to get there. It was a cul-de-sac. Knew the neighbor to the left, and another two to the right. Except him!

* * *

It's been two years since we had the privilege of serving M & W on their way to enjoying their new adventures in Colorado.

THANK YOU, Top Secret Santa! We've yet to meet, but we are deeply grateful, just the same. Your secret is safe with us.

Have My Cake And Eat It Too

S told me she was the original pastry chef for this famous Filipino bakery. And every time I'd visit and catch her home, there was no way I was leaving without some real goodies.

Now that she was retired, she spent her time and talent baking these little tasty treats for her church and others.

Out of the blue, I get a call around mid-morning:

"Hi Jack, it's S. Can you stop by our house later? I have a mango cake for you."

What??? I haven't savored THIS mango cake in years. And it is one of my favorites, from childhood on.

I was in for another surprise. Turns out she didn't make me a mini-cake. It was a full-sized work of baked art.

"I remembered it was one of your favorites, and since I had all the right ingredients, I thought I'd make you one. You have to drive home slowly so it doesn't wobble, and have to let it set in the fridge for another six hours. Enjoy, Jack!"

Six HOURS? That might make this poor mango crazy!

* * *

L, I'm so touched, and so thankful for your delicious generosity. You also made my birthday really special, as we were just sticking a candle on a doughnut this year, thanks to covid. And it was way beyond good.

August 25

Bad Error Day

One of the things I never comment on is anyone's – hair.

It can be a touchy subject. Surrounded by four females, I should know.

Every morning, I see my own casualties from the previous night, short black strands littered all over, lying motionless, my pillowcase for a graveyard.

To this day I don't know why I said what I said. Never realized my stupidity could be so endlessly deep.

One of the most practical solutions I've implemented, is a nine-second delay in all my text and email communications.

No such safety net for my mouth, though.

As I greeted X, this just hurtled out of me:

"Hey, you look different."

What the follicle did I just say? I could've shut up. Had my chance. It gets worse.

"Uh, I mean, do you have a different hairdo?"

"Ugh. I'm so sorry! I'm so sorry! I don't know why I even said that. I'm so sorry!"

My tongue needed a trim and a bleach. And a lashing.

YOUR Page

Many of you asked: "What will it take to get in your book?", so I'm implementing THE craziest idea I heard that excited me.

And really scared me.

First, the BIG fine print. To keep my CPA and attorney happy, there are no financial, copyright, intellectual, commercial or any other rights that I owe you for any submissions. All submissions are final. I reserve the exclusive right to include (or not include) submissions for any reason. This can be changed, or ended, for any reason, at any time. You hold me harmless for any consequences. By submitting, you AGREE to all stated stipulations, and subsequent amendments, if any.

All the above will likely never apply to 99.99% of you. So let's have some fun. If you've had an episode with me, be it good, bad or best yet, funny, that you HONESTLY BELIEVE CAN BE **UPLIFTING**, send it to *jack@91709jack.com*.

Your FIRST name will be published. Despite the above fine print, assume your submission will be posted AS IS. Be careful in mentioning SOMEONE ELSE by name. THOUSANDS may read what you write. NO profanity, but OK, you be "creative."

jackddd.com/yourpage

September 4

Cirque du Chino Hills

First time we could afford to watch Cirque du Soleil, our cheap tickets behind a pole made acrobats of my eyes and neck.

They have amazing jugglers, but I know they can't keep fifteen or more plates of spinning escrows in the air and not drop a single one. Lauren can. On top of a husband and two boys.

It's an epic task to have every detail and moving part under the big tent go as smoothly as possible. Things can, and do go haywire. Escrows have fallen from dangerous heights. Listings have expired. John is our master of the real estate tightrope, walking it for nearly 20 years. Good for him, because I'm REALLY afraid of heights. He's got lion-taming down too.

Marketing duties fall on my shoulders. I'll never stop working to find ways to attract the best audience for your listing. I've eaten a lot of glass and interesting brown stuff over the years.

Of her many roles, we love Michelle for writing the checks. Queen over the kitchen, with her army of coffee makers and creamers, one of her finest acts involve lady fingers and knife skills, when she slices and serves her killer tiramisu.

With one trick up his armpits, Cooper performs fist bumps.

Their cat, Maggie, can walk around with a "No Littering" sign.

Brandon alone volunteered for the water tank, as no one knew what was swimming in it until it was ShowingTime. He has been snuggled by goldfish, zapped by eels, ignored by a few others, and eaten by sharks. Somehow, he has managed to climb out alive every time, ready for another dive.

There have been a few times when John & I have held our breaths watching one of his performances.

I've been blessed with my wonderful son-in-law, Sam. Now, I even have a son-in-awe, Brandon. Super proud of you!

Many acts pack up on a truck and bounce from city to city, but not us. We're your one-town troupe - our pegs, tents, hearts and souls permanently bolted down here in Chino Hills.

And that clown getting chased by flame-spitting fire eaters before the show? That's my side gig.

If any of us were forced into the ring, the only one who could put on a real show would be John & Michelle's youngest daughter, Madison, who is involved in some scary, competitive level cheer and tumbling.

* * *

Don't know how I rounded all of us into a circus. But what we do takes a lot of skill, and can be dangerous. And we always stick together. If it sounds like I'm bragging on them, YES I AM.

Was *really* tempted to make John the juggler, since he could easily toss lots of Balsz in the air.

P.S. Want a peek at the promo poster in progress? WHO should be the bearded lady?

It's at Jackddd.com/poster

September 7

Purple Brick(ed)

There was already ANOTHER agent's Supra at the front door handle.

"Oh, THAT. I'll let my wife tell you guys the story," said X.

Y doesn't mess around. She knows her numbers. And when she gets going, you best hang on.

"The Purple Brick agent said, 'Not only can I do it cheaper than anyone, I got more sales than anyone.' Apparently he was so confident I'd pick him, he had the nerve to leave that lockbox on our door! Warned him he better take it off in a few days, or I'm sawing it off and tossing it.

(Turns out the company was spending millions in ads, and funneling it to ONE agent covering San Bernardino AND Riverside, more than 17 cities. Not long after they went BK.)

Then there's this agent Q, who kept pushing and pushing my husband, not knowing I'm the one who makes the decision.

Jack, on the other hand, you never once pushed. X likes you. Heck, even I like you. We trust you both will do for us what you've done for all your Chino Hills clients! You're hired!"

* * *

X & Y, we're so happy to have set a record for you, $100,000 over the previous comp. While it was a challenge, we knew how to defend and fight for you. Many happy years ahead as you suffer by the beach!

Ding DOG!

For years, all the ding dongs never gave me the chance to meet them.

Turning around to leave, I didn't expect to hear the front door creak open.

In our newsletter months earlier, something caught her eye.

"Hi Jack! I'm H, so nice to meet you! Remember when you had the picture of the bulldog puppy in your arms? His dad used to be my son's dog! I guess you know R, the new owner too! What a small world!"

*

When I visited R a few months later, a lady I didn't recognize was standing outside.

"Who are you?" she inquired.

"Oh, I'm Jack. I know R. And the dogs too."

"Well, that's Vito sitting in front of you. That's strange – he's acting like he knows you."

"No way! He was the size of a fat salami when I cuddled him in my arms a few months back. He grew FAST. He got big."

Showed her the picture too.

Of course I had to give both father and son bulldogs some love and attention. As they dripped and slathered some on me.

September 9

I've Not Been Naughty

Not talking about Big Red Jolly Guy.

I concluded there was no such person from the North Pole from an early age, because I saw my Mom bring the presents home through the front door (not the chimney), saw HER wrap them all up and pile it under the tree, and SHE handed them to us. Oh, I also recognized her handwriting on the little gift cards.

That, or maybe SHE was Santa Claus.

*

"You better not be thinking of doing any hanky-panky around town," said Q.

Of course I wouldn't!

I was afraid to ask what she meant.

"All your wife would have to do is simply go on Chino Hills Connections, and post,

'Where's Jack?'

and we'd have your car and exact location pretty quickly. That, or a few thousand people would be on the lookout to turn you in."

* * *

How nice…I think?

September 14

Illegal

As hard as John & I compete, we will also bow out graciously.

Having just lost one, it was back on the market in days, with another agent. All the best, just the same.

No matter how brutal the sport, there are rules. Even the Mafia has them, at least from the movies I've watched.

> Here's one of the MOST important ethical and compliance rules, under California CRMLS, Section 12.4: Basically,
>
> **Until a listing is officially cancelled, or expired, as entered on the Multiple Listing Service, NO AGENT can solicit that seller.**

Turns out their new agent was from outside the area. The surprise characteristic of his listings? ALL five were cancelled weeks before. *(As of January, 2021, it's 12 of 13, with 4 sold.)*

Here are two major possibilities:

(1) Sellers do their research, decide to call (PERFECTLY OK) an agent who has NEVER marketed in any way in our city. Or,

(2) Agent contacts sellers DURING the active listing period.

Knowing how much time, effort and money it takes to brand and still be barely remembered makes (1) a long shot in the dark. And (2) is always ileegal. I'll leave it at that.

(Should you ever choose to list, please support an honest agent of your choice who at the very least, works by the rules.)

September 16

Heartmelt

As I was visiting with K, I see their two daughters waving, and disappearing. Before I left, they came back, and had a little present for me.

There's M & A's three amazing children, who have all impressively learned a foreign language. But from the first time I met them, I could see they were first taught the language of love, kindness and joy.

Then S & L's daughters, and so many more, who have called me by name from a very young age.

One thing no one prepared me for, was how many times over the years my heart would get melted into a puddle.

* * *

J & K, M & A, S & L, your precious children ALWAYS make my day 1,000 times brighter than sunshine!

And that goes for so many more of you and your children, who have blessed my heart to overflowing. THANK YOU for feeding my soul.

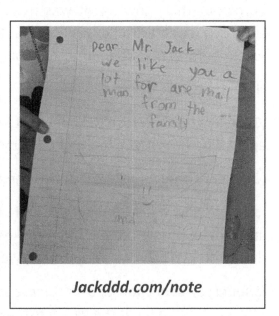

Jackddd.com/note

September 17

Where There's A Wheel, There's A Way

In the years I've known this spunky, positive force of joy, through the pain of losing her husband D much too early, to her ongoing MS challenges, she always found a reason why every day is a gift from God that was made just for her.

One late Friday, S called, crying on the phone. She decided not to sell her home, and felt bad as we had already geared up for multiple weekend showings. I gently reassured her consider it done, no worries, and she didn't owe us a thing.

S then tells me the new home builder refused to return her two deposit checks, despite promises they would, asking if I had any ideas to help her.

After emailing me her details, with nothing to lose, a "friendly" letter in her name was composed. With her smile, signature and a prayer, we FedExed it straight to the CEO. Within a week, she had good news that his office called, apologized, and would promptly send her money back.

Her neighbors around her – YOU are all love and care in motion, taking turns checking in on S, several times a day, always there for her, seventeen years and counting.

* * *

S, you are an inspiration to me, and I'm certain to anyone who is fortunate enough to be touched by you when their paths intersect the lane of your life. We'll all be cheering you on when your wheel power takes a back seat to your will power.

September 18

Nice Jack

M decides to borrow his neighbor's jack. Since his hands were full, I volunteered my chicken wing biceps to carry two little parts.

As we walked to his home, M remarked that it was really great that he got to use this helpful, hardworking, and really nice jack.

In case you were wondering, it's the blue thing to the left.

Not sure about the thing on the right.

Jackddd.com/nice

He Said, She Said

Here are some of the most interesting things YOU said about the first *Ding Dong Diaries*. There's good, there's funny, and of course, there's, well... you'll see. THANK YOU!

"And I thought I was special. Until I saw my neighbors had one too!" CP

"They weren't all funny. Three of them made me cry. So I sat my family down and read those to them." KS

"I told my kids to buy me the book for my birthday!" DL

"I love it, Jack! I've made it required reading, even if someone's NOT in real estate. As a matter of fact, we have our copy here at the house, and also a copy at each of our two vacation homes." DW

"Perfect timing! My husband had knee surgery yesterday, and he's out for three months!" AL

"I took the book to work to read during my lunch, and someone ran off with it. I was hoping they'd read it and bring it back, but no luck. They must have really enjoyed it." YK

"No, didn't read it, sure felt like I did. Every time my wife read something funny, she'd come over and read me the page." SM

"M started reading your book and hasn't put it down...lol. Every once in a while he gets a smile on his face... And I packed that book, thinking I was going to read it on our vacation." RA

"Can we buy another copy of your Diaries book please? Our son accidentally spilled coffee on the copy you dropped off, and our other son would like his own copy without the coffee stains. Oh, and we already found OUR story in the book!" KK

"I'm packing for a cruise, and saved your book for it." DK

"I really only know my five neighbors. You just showed me we live in a city of beautiful people and families." RC

"On our 4-hour road trip, we took turns reading your book aloud to ourselves and our kids! It was a blast!" MJ

"After the last few months, I can use the comic relief." GS

"...This morning I thumbed through the first few pages, figuring I'd get back to it someday. I just finished reading it. Got quite a few chuckles out of it, maybe even a tear. Or two. A great way to spend my Sunday morning..." SM

"I have to put it down so I can get stuff done because it is habit forming! SO upbeat and positive that it is a joy to read!" RL

"Can I buy another copy? It's a gift for a dear friend. I know she'll love it because she has a strange sense of humor." SX

"No. Didn't read it. Threw in the trash. At least I'm honest." ZZ

Lastly, you'll just have to watch Fernando's comments on video at *Jackddd.com/comments*

September 19

Once Open A Time

One of the highlights we snorted as a family, was the stench of the Titan Arum, the world's biggest (and stinkiest) flower. It blooms once every nine years, usually just for one day.

For sixty-two months, I never encountered a soul. And that evil voice in your head says, "Maybe just give up on this one stinker of a door. There are so many others."

But I didn't. I never have.

I was on the way next door when I heard the front door open.

"Jack! I wanted to catch you last time but you already left! Come on in. I'm T."

"My in-laws, M & M, they know you too." he said.

With their three grown children all doing well, it was time for T and his wife, N, to enjoy the fruit of their labors.

"I've seen you several times before, but keep missing you. Always read your flyers. You're different. I wanted to make sure I caught you the next time. I normally don't open our door. But for some reason, something made me decide to talk to you. We're thinking of selling, and have some questions."

* * *

T & N, THANK YOU for the opportunity to serve you, literally putting your home in escrow while you were out of town! May you have many long, healthy and happy years ahead.

September 25

You're Not Sneaking Out Of Here

Months earlier, I caught D rushing out. V just had a stroke...

On my next drop by, not wanting to disturb them, I intended to leave the latest update under their mat — when the front door suddenly swings open as their caretaker left.

"Well, hello, Jack!" D greeted.

"I'm so sorry. Didn't even want to disturb you. How is V?"

"Come on in, and greet him yourself! You're NOT sneaking out of here, are you? My husband loves seeing you."

As we head to the living room, D tells V, "Honey, guess who I found at the front door?"

After turning over slowly in his bed, V greeted me with his warm smile. I was smiling too, but couldn't help but tear up.

"See what I mean? I told you!" said D.

He reminisced about a full life lived. D, who was a nurse, took such good care of V that his progress would surprise doctors.

He enjoyed the view of green hills and blue skies, sipping his orange juice.

* * *

When D told me V had passed, another hole was punched into my heart. There is sadness, but it's also filled with wonderful moments you both blessed me with. THANK YOU always.

New York City, FL 91709

A text comes in at 3:46 PM. All it said was,

"Hi Jack, we are in NYC and ran into this beautiful young woman."

"What?" I thought. Then I see the picture.

How could an old client of ours who moved to Florida be standing next to my eldest daughter in New York City?!?

B & B, who are great patrons of theatre, were investors in a show where my daughter did the costumes!

As they chatted, B mentioned they retired to Florida, after living in Chino Hills, California, for decades.

My daughter goes, "No way. I grew up in Chino Hills! Say, my dad knows a lot of people in town. Maybe you know him? His name is Jack. Jack Soliman?"

"You have got to me kidding me. Awww, my wife and I love Jack. Known him over the years. Your dad and his partner were the ones who sold our Chino Hills home!"

"We need to take a picture, send it to your dad and freak him out right now!"

They did. They sure did!

B & B, miss your warmth and humor! Wishing you both many happy Floridian days and nights, less the hurricanes.

September 28

Dear Abby: Is It Ever OK To Hug Someone...

...I've only met a few times? Who's beautiful, sweet and adorable? Whose parents know I'm married, and were OK? And with practically the same name as my wife?

Well, I took a chance and I did. Got pictures to prove it.

Even told my wife about her. Meet Heidi!

Thank you, J & J, for your permission!

*

Speaking of my wife's name, Hedy, how's this?

S has been a volunteer for training guide dogs for years.

Jackddd.com/Heidi

(Personally I can't imagine how hard it must be for anyone to love a lab or retriever pup from birth to two years, then have to let it go, even for such a worthy cause.)

One of them was named Heddie.

Then she told me the name of her first dog was Mimi. I told her that's what our girls call my wife.

Heady stuff!

Sorry, You're NOT Jack!

John & Laurie* decided to list with a close relative, despite her never selling a home in Chino Hills. Within days, they realized there was going to be NO plan, NO follow-up, and NO marketing to any buyers, Asian or otherwise. But they were stuck with her for months.

Next they chose an Asian agent from another city, who promised easy offers above market value from overseas buyers. Again, nothing happened.

The day the listing expired, I stopped by. John then yells with a big laugh, "Honey, guess who finally showed up!"

"Is it Jack?" Laurie answered from upstairs.

"Ok, Jack. Listing's yours. But I have a story for you."

He told me he'd been sitting by the door, as agents from all over dropped by with promises that would embarrass Pinocchio and fry lie detectors.

He told all of them, 'Oops, sorry. You're NOT Jack.'

And to those who asked, "Jack who?" his response just cracked me up...

"If you don't know Jack, then you really don't know jack about selling my home, because you're not even from here. Bye!"

It still wasn't easy. Our first buyer cancelled, but we were able to get a great new offer.

SOLD! Hello Vegas!

* * *

They were gracious enough to allow me to print their names and share their experience.

We have always been willing to tell the truth, even if it meant losing a potential client. We honestly pointed out challenges, AND presented a strategy. The other agents brushed aside the issue, both times telling them we did NOT know what we were doing.

And here's the screenshot of their text to me. (It's unretouched, except for making the print bigger.)

John & Laurie, Congratulations as you retire and enjoy your beautiful new home. THANK YOU for your kindness and humor over the years, and the privilege of serving you.

Even if we had to wait, standing third in line.

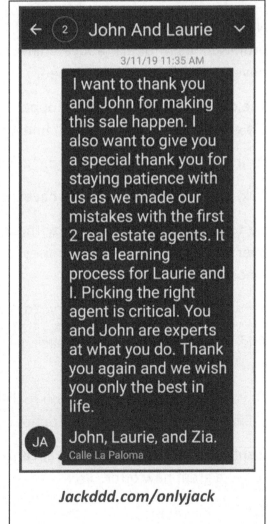

John And Laurie

3/11/19 11:35 AM

I want to thank you and John for making this sale happen. I also want to give you a special thank you for staying patience with us as we made our mistakes with the first 2 real estate agents. It was a learning process for Laurie and I. Picking the right agent is critical. You and John are experts at what you do. Thank you again and we wish you only the best in life.

JA John, Laurie, and Zia.
Calle La Paloma

Jackddd.com/onlyjack

October 6

Belly Rub

As an essential business, John & I never stopped taking care of our clients throughout 2020. Observing safety precautions for all parties involved, our appointments and required meetings continued.

On March 15, I decided to temporarily suspend my personal visits.

I resumed making my rounds on July 15, taking and respecting necessary precautions, of course.

It was really good to see many of you again, thankful to find pretty much all of you healthy.

As M opened their front door, before we could say much, their dog Penny makes a bee line for me, and flops on her back.

"No belly rub, no talking to my humans," she seemed to say by her happy barks.

"Well, we missed you, Jack. And Penny missed you too!"

It was time to start getting more dog hair on.

* * *

So nice to see you, M! And Penny of course.

October 8

Bungled Book

"Jack, you free tomorrow? Guess what, need to put our home on the market as soon as possible. Fill you in when you get here."

After all these years, I finally met T, R's wife. "Hi, T! Can't believe I'm saying 'Hi,' and have to follow it with 'Bye!'"

By the door, T goes, "I got a little something to pick with you."

Gulp. What could it be?

"I'm at work, and I happen to have a coworker who also lives in Chino Hills. I didn't tell her we were thinking of selling, but asked if she knew you. Told her I've never met you, but according to my husband, you've sold a lot, and were a really nice guy.

Well, of course she said she knew who you were, and had similar positive comments. Then my coworker added, 'As a matter of fact, he wrote this funny book called the *Ding Dong Diaries*, and even autographed our copy for us! Have you read it?'

When I came home, I asked my husband if we ever got one. 'Don't think so,' he said."

I felt like a flat tire. And even though my car never came equipped with a spare tire, it usually has a spare *book*. Or two.

* * *

R & T, congratulations on your dream home, and THANK YOU!

If any of you in Chino Hills never got my book, it's NOT intentional. Please ask for your free autographed copy.

October 12

My Smile Is Bigger Than My Black Eye

While it shouldn't be a surprise we fight hard for the chance to serve you, please always know we respect your decision. You owe us no explanation, much less any apology. Whatever John & I can learn from our shortcomings, we welcome that.

When I have a down moment, this is a 5,000 mg capsule of kindness available to me without a prescription, with no negative side effects.

(Other than personal details, reproduced here in its entirety.)

*

Hi Jack,

My name is S, and I live at XYZ Street. I wanted to let you know that we are listing our house (maybe today) with a different realtor, but I needed to tell you why. You have always been so warm and wonderful coming around the neighborhood and I really did want to contact you.

However this whole process started out as a fluke and went farther than I thought it ever would. You see, we had truly intended to relocate to ABC area but were never really looking forward to it and so we weren't looking very hard.

Then one day we were driving to Harkins Theaters and saw an open house sign and decided to stop by. The neighborhood was one I always loved. Well my family ended up loving the house and now we have an offer in on it contingent on our selling our house in the next 14 days! Since it was an X listing my husband just felt it was easier to do the entire process with X.

Anyway, I just wanted you to hear it from me and not just see the listing. And believe me, after what we've been through in the process so far, I'm kicking myself for not calling you first.

If you want to come by this weekend and see the house yourself, feel free to stop by.

Thanks for being a wonderful neighbor and overall great guy!

S

* * *

I have a priceless collection of emails, cards, scraps, notes, pictures, voicemails and text messages from many of you that have blessed me in ways I will never be able to repay.

The times we get knocked down hard, the details get sent to my lemonade factory, and I just move on. But the smiles you bring never go away.

P.S. Fifteen months later, I got another email with only THREE words in the title. It simply said, "Ready to sell."

S & P, THANK YOU always for the privilege of serving you. And for that gracious note permanently stuck in the inbox of my heart.

No Sales

6:48 PM

Met M for the first time, as he parked his car in his garage.

"Nice to meet you, Jack," said M, taking a glance at my flyer.

"I'm impressed you're out here working this late. Perfectly understand if you had no sales, and you had to make something happen. But even more impressed that you're out here, with a list of sales like that. And you look like you're having a blast!"

THANK YOU, M for the very kind encouragement.

* * *

One thing that sets successful people apart, is their devotion to their craft AFTER achieving success. DESPITE is an even better word, because it's so much easier to let off the gas and cruise.

I'm not for 24/7 focus at the expense of family or health. But magic happens when one shows up for practice AFTER you've "made it," however you define it.

In my relatively short career in real estate, my Chino Hills volume has crossed $212 million. In opportunities to share with other agents, I remind them the moment they "arrive" is just that, a literal fleeting second. True fulfillment comes from finding meaning and joy from the journey – which is 99.9% of it. I also confess that none of my butterflies ever left, and there's more of them now. They don't even fly in formation when I want them to. My secret? I do it anyways. Only then do they flap in a line, behind me. Most of them, anyway.

October 12

What Husband?

Sometimes it would take years before I get to meet the better half. While a few have gone sideways, most go very nicely.

But this is something else.

Ding dong.

The front door opens, and I'm met with a warm smile.

"Hi! You must be P's husband?" I asked.

> *"Actually, NO…and I need to hurry up because HE will be home SOON."*

What was I supposed to say? I didn't even know where to look.

*

He waited a few moments, seemingly savoring my uneasiness, which P seemed to notice as she came to the front door.

"I'm N, by the way. And I was just kidding. Very nice meeting you, Jack. I AM the husband. My wife has spoken very highly of you."

We're both laughing as P steps out.

"*WHAT* did you tell him???"

Police Sit Down

When an officer asks me to have a seat, I comply.

"Jack, I consider you a friend, and I have something to tell you. Just found out I have 14 months to live. I've had a wonderful life, a beautiful family."

In moments like this, time stops. Felt like my heart did too.

"And I'm very grateful. You see, a close friend went to Vegas less than two weeks ago, and never came back. And I get to see and hug and love my wife and kids every single day."

The next time I saw him, S told me with a hearty laugh, "I'm a cockroach, because I'm tough and indestructible."

I happened to catch them coming home one late afternoon. S slowly gets out of their car. Got the chance to give him a hug, wishing him well, as we laughed and cried.

Never thought that would be the last time I'd see him.

As difficult as it was, I was somehow allowed to watch a man's man go through ups and downs, pain and uncertainty, with courage, contentment and even humor. Above all, he fought with grace and gratitude.

* * *

S, that conversation we had, as we sat next to each other by that shaded tree will always stay with me. Rest in peace, kind and mighty friend. To P, may S's love always surround you and your family. THANK YOU to all of you, for sharing your lives with me.

October 13

You Know Jack Too?

"What happened to 'I'll be right back'?" my wife asks, after the projected in-and-out Costco run turned into an hour and a half.

"Well, of course Daddy got stopped by more people," my daughters would tell my wife. Chick Fil-A, bank, gas station, even almost every place we eat in town. It's always fun to run in to all of you. (Except when my memory sputters...)

At this one crowded event, I was going to plant myself at the first available chair.

Spotting one, I asked the lady if it was free.

She looks up, and goes, "Oh my gosh! Hi, Jack! Here, sit down!"

As I greeted her, the gentleman next to him rears his head, and he goes, "Well, hello there, Jack! Nice to see you again."

Then the couple looked at **each other**, and said, "YOU know Jack too?"

We all had a great time.

And this wasn't the only time something like that happened.

* * *

Well, I knew both of them when they were in their previous relationships. We all know things happen for many reasons. It was great to see them – they made a very nice couple, and I'm very happy for them.

Life Depends On You

As D's health took a weak turn, I was invited to stop by. There was a lot of food, family and friends. Yes, tears. And LOVE.

"Go ahead, Jack. YELL. Make sure he hears you," S, his wife, shouted over the din. He opened his eyes for a moment, and I had a chance to thank him one more time, and pray with him.

D was bigger than life. In fact, I used to be *scared* of him. He told me weird stories and jokes, delivering punchlines with a scowl, leaving me unsure whether to laugh or not. A few years back, he shared this deeply personal and difficult episode in his life.

"Jack, I wasted years, because I got depressed and sat at home when I had to start using adult diapers. Years! Missed my golf, going out with S, but what really got me was not being a part of my grandkids' lives when they came. I really quit on life, on me.

When I decided to stop feeling sorry for myself, and just put those darn things on, you know what? I got my life back. Just like that. And now, I LOVE them. You have my permission to tell my diaper story to encourage someone else."

True to form, he started laughing, like the D I've always known.

* * *

News of D passing away peacefully came just a few days later. D, you were the toughest guy I knew, golfing till the end. S, we'll miss you, but so happy you left Chino Hills to be with the kids and grandkids. So much love and fond memories of you & D. The precious honor is truly, truly mine.

October 20

How Much Is That Doggie In The Big Cage?

How much is that doggie in the big cage?
Why doesn't it have a waggly tail?
Are you sure it's really a doggie in the big cage?
I'm not sure that's a doggie up for sale!

Over several visits, J would show me the latest cool remodel or upgrade to their home. One time, boxes were stacked all the way to the ceiling.

This time, most were gone. Except for this big cage. A REALLY BIG one. It was for a Great Dane. Never seen one that massive, so I had to snap a picture of it.

Then J suggests, "Want me to take a picture of you INSIDE it?"

Always a willing volunteer, "Of course!" I said.

Sadly, it fits me rather comfortably. For free food and lodging...might not be a bad idea.

Jackddd.com/cage

A Little Social MEdia

Thanks to a busy schedule, I'm rarely on social media. But to every one of you who have taken your time to post a picture, and type out a comment or two about me, I'm truly humbled.

Text messages will roll in, telling me I better go have a look.

"This man is Brilliant!!! Jack Soliman...the funny real estate agent that drives around in a little red car, knocking on doors and personally getting to know the people in the community. We just love when he visits, and now...he left us a book!?!?!"

After that gracious post from J, is a trail of dozens upon dozens of super nice comments.

THANK YOU SO MUCH, J!

*

Another time a couple and I were catching up at Take Ur Seat. (*GREAT people and food!*) They ask what I'd been up to lately.

"Wanna see something funny?" I offered.

"Hey, I wanna see something funny," our server chimed in.

Showing them a picture of my Jackbrella, our server goes, "Hey, just saw that. Hang on."

"...saw it posted on Chino Hills Connections. Here, see? Lots and lots of comments and likes!"

THANK YOU SO MUCH, Another J!

October 24

Driver License, Please

Turning off a busy street, I park my car to check on some messages.

As I scroll through them, I see a motorcycle officer come up the street from behind me. Nothing unusual.

Until I hear two knocks on my driver's side window.

Through the proverbial slow motion mental rewind, I convinced myself I wasn't speeding, and did not make an illegal turn of any sort. Tags are current.

What could IT be?

"Driver license, please," the officer firmly requested.

"Hi officer. Here you go…"

Before I could ask why, he started to laugh out loud.

"Jack! Buddy! I GOT you! You should've seen your face!"

I see his last name on his uniform.

"For sure, T! You almost scared the daylights out of me!"

"I'll let you off this time. Just make sure you get us the house we want."

Even The Brave Get Scared

Q & I always had interesting conversations, from her favorite piece of custom stained glass adorning one of her windows, to memorabilia steeped in cherished moments over the years.

As we sat on her kitchen table, she tells me she's scared.

"When my husband first developed Alzheimer's years ago, I knew nothing about it, and so I studied up on it."

She did everything to care for him, till she physically could not.

"Jack, I thinking about getting myself screened for it. As much as I hate to admit it, I'm seeing signs of it in me. I'm scared."

My heart was crushed as she silently wept in front of me.

Months later, Q told me the tests confirmed her worst fears.

*

"Hi Jack, this is Q's daughter. You don't know me, but I know Mom is very fond of you. I have some bad news, as her Alzheimer's has taken a very swift turn for the worse.

By the way, we want to thank you again for Mom's Ring doorbell. It has kept the bad guys out, but it's kept Mom safely in the house. We catch her every time she tries to sneak out!"

* * *

Q, I'll always remember your wit, kindness and courage. So honored to spend time with you, and serve you over the years.

October 25

Going To Church

Wrapping up the paperwork for our new sellers, G & G, they said they were getting ready to go to church.

On the way out, I asked if I could use their bathroom.

Didn't realize I was going to church too.

Pillow

While I use one every night, I never thought I'd BECOME one.

"Don't move!" said P, as she pointed to the floor.

Lexie was flat on her back, then decided my left shoe would make a nice pillow. It was certainly softer than the floor, so she made herself very comfortable for a while.

Jackddd.com/pillow

She made sure we had eye contact, as if to say, "Look at me. Don't even think of moving."

That was too adorable.

* * *

I watched lots of samurai movies growing up.

Never forgot the first time I saw them sleeping on wooden BLOCKS. Those were pillows, alright, but should be pronounced more like pill-OW – to rhyme with 'cow.' That's my contribution to the list of confusing exceptions to English pronunciation rules.

October 27

Cinco de Mayo

Not "Mayo" the month, but "mayo" that glues your bread together.

P has a green thumb, and everything he touches flourishes. He grows his own herbs and greens. Turns out he's quite the foodie, so we dove into the deep end of a delicious discussion.

Among other things, I'm plastered when he tells me some of the ingredients in many popular canned soups are used to make PAINT.

(Judging from the gallons I've ingested in my youth, my insides should have a semi-gloss coat of cream of mushroom.)

On a more enviable note, his job requires him to taste all sorts of things. He was paid to savor (then usually spit out) the finest morsels of Belgian chocolate, in my humble opinion, the most important vegetable. (Alas, "choc" that one to history – he chucked that position.)

His taste buds still pay the bills. Sessions currently last two to four hours, and he often does them back-to-back. Lately, he has been discerning the subtle differences of textures and flavors of up to *cinco de* mayo!

Actually, it's more than five.

Make that TWENTY-FOUR globs.

I'm sure he does a *'naise* job.

God ~~Bless~~ You

(All fingers point at me first. But for the grace of God, go I. And while we're at it, how about a candid confession?

The first draft had funny stories that were way too mean. With seeds and rind thrown in, the sip was bitter. Demon-ade. Served myself humble pie, and re-squeezed a new batch with just the right touch of sweetness.

This was one of them.)

Having not seen them in a while, I waved as I saw their car approaching in their neck of the woods.

I see the car slow down, the window roll down. Then I got a beat down.

"DON'T EVER COME TO OUR HOME AGAIN! DON'T EVER LEAVE YOUR FLYERS AGAIN!"

Stunned, I watched the vehicle drive away, with a decal that could have read, "God BLAST You!"

What's that saying again..."Stickers and stones can break my bones..."

* * *

It's why I DON'T have stickers, except Cooper's face. Because you know, it's sad, but true - I can be a jerk too. And when I act like one, I'm sorry.

To you, whatever it is that got you so upset, I apologize.

October 29

He Doesn't Need One

B was a gentle giant, who always welcomed me with a big smile. Even through the most difficult days, they'd have me come in and visit him, even bedside. Those were tough, but precious and treasured times I'll never forget.

The news I hope to never receive came, that he had passed away peacefully. There was going to be a celebration of his life, and friends asked if I could attend. That's the least I could do to honor his memory.

The place was packed, the message was beautiful, and the video of his life was really something else.

On the way out, they handed directions to B & K's home for refreshments. As a lady handed me one, another lady startles me by YANKING it out of my hands, laughing as she explains:

"He doesn't need one. He knows where they live. Jack knows where I live. He knows where a LOT of people live!"

I hope B would approve of such a moment, as it reminded me of his sense of humor.

* * *

Not long after, two others said they saw the whole exchange, and said to themselves, "Yeah, he knows where WE live too!"

To B, no more sorrow, no more pain, joy forevermore in the presence of our Lord Jesus Christ! See you again. To K, He will always keep you, and wrap His arms of love around you.

Fit For A King

It's no surprise I've caught so many of you doing all sorts of things when I show up unannounced.

Watching a movie, napping, working, playing, yelling, fighting, cleaning, and more.

With advances in technology, many of you have used your Ring or other video doorbells to screen the latest uninvited visitor.

Like X did.

We chatted for a few minutes over his Ring doorbell, as it was the first time I "met" him.

After telling me where he was, he still carried on an actual conversation with me.

X, I really appreciate you taking the time for me.

For that, you should be seated on a throne.

Because you were seated on a throne.

We just need to get you a crown that fits.

* * *

THANK YOU, X. You know I appreciate you!

November 1

Chino Hillarious

Yes, we take our business and clients most seriously. But when it comes to myself, I don't.

You also know almost nothing will offend me, so I get excited when you ask me if I'd like to hear something perilously funny.

I'm of the firm belief that when it comes to comedy, riddles, laughter, wit and jokes, any sort of correctness, political, social, religious or otherwise, should be dumped at the door.

God is no laughing matter. But one can't ignore His cosmic sense of humor when He created the egg-laying platypus, and baby-squirting daddy seahorse, just to name a few.

Of the gems that have had me braying like a donkey, one stands at the top. Unfortunately, it is wrong on so many levels, I can't even get myself to publicly put it down in writing, much less repeat. It is appropriately witty, tying both American and Chinese cultures, two little lines enough to fit on a fortune cookie. That's all I'll ever say about it.

This page will self-destruct in 5. 4. 3. 2. 1. Poof!

Still here? Too bad!

PLEASE keep your funny slices of life coming my way.

Hahahahahaha.

Where's The ~~Beef~~ Fish?

Fish stories. We've all heard them - "Mine's THIS big." Fortunately, in our line of work, there IS a registry that records every fish that anyone has ever caught, called the Multiple Listing Service.

Getting ready to list B & D's home, he said,

"I've always wondered about THAT."

THAT is the whale of a tale of the number of sales some agents have used as bait, and even proclaim in print, often missing a crucial disclaimer or two, such as: whether or not they caught their fish from one pond or seventeen lakes, or if they caught all that fish by themselves or with a group of thirteen.

Usually though, as B simply put, "Did they really do all THAT?"

"Don't ask me. Want to see what the MLS says?" I offer.

We simply log on, enter their first and last names, and the fish count is plain as a shark has teeth.

"Six in the last year?" laughs B.

Not at the other agent's numbers, but because he's still holding our "accordion" of results.

You'll never smell a fishy story from us. We make it easy for you to inspect our catch we've toiled very hard for. Off the MLS, or right off our boat. We'll always show you OUR fish. (FYI: List of ALL our catch on pages 221 – 231.)

November 9

reFEARrals

"Hi Jack. My name is J. You don't know me, but I asked my best friend who I should call to sell our home. She said you, and that's good enough. I trust her and we go way back. When are you free?"

I have received many calls just like that. It has always hit me the same way.

There's the happy adrenalin for a split second.

Then astonishment, surprise, a sprinkling of shock, wrapped in a giant hug of gratefulness. And then –

FEAR.

You read that correctly.

It is a good fear, of a tremendous responsibility that has been handed to me as a privilege.

Because you have entrusted someone you care about to me.

And the precious relationship you have with your family, friend or loved one.

John & I know we WILL do a good job. But knowing so many of you have thought of us, we want you all to know there are not enough words to express how much we appreciate you.

* * *

THANK YOU, my Chino Hills families. Yes, YOU!

Social Distancing

This was BEFORE the 6-feet kind with masks.

I confess to hardly spending much time on social media, like Facebook and its various mutations.

I'm very social, just not on those media. I prefer Facelook.

May I ask a ~~little~~ GIANT favor from all of you?

Should you wake up one day and have even the most microscopic reason to get a hold of me, please, PLEASE –

Text, call, or email. Leave a note on my car. Wave me down. Call a friend. Google will even tell you I got arrested AND give you my number (QR code and link below).

Anything but leave a DM on Facebook Messenger...

"Would like to discuss my house, but don't want to meet at my house due to (reason). Will you be available on Monday?"

I blame no one but myself. By the time I saw it thirty-three DAYS later, the home was already listed with someone else.

Prefer prompt replies? 909-262-3132 really works. In case you're in the mood for aging your message like wine, TikTok might work, as I don't even have an account.

Kidding aside, kindly call or text. Neither bite.

* * *

Jackddd.com/arrested

November 12

To Be, Or Not Too Bee?

Are some cultures more sensitive to "unlucky" numbers?

"Hey, Jack, I heard some Asian buyers don't like house numbers ending in a '4.' Why is that?"

"You know how we have different words in English that sound the same, but are spelled differently - like 'four,' 'fore' and 'for'? (*They're called homophones.*) In Chinese, there are also different characters that almost sound the same. The number '4' sounds like the character for 'death' (though with different tones), and that's where the association comes from."

While he wasn't bothered in the least by this, when asked how he felt if we changed his number to '666,' well, that was a *'different'* situation, he reasoned.

Most in the Western world don't have the warm and fuzzies for '666,' thanks to religious beliefs, or getting scarred and scared by watching "The Omen" movies.

The first time we listed a home with '666' on the address, John was curious how that was going to affect things.

"Well, the same people who don't care for '4,' LIKE the '6,' because it sounds like the character for 'happy' or 'happiness.' And this isn't just one happy. We got TRIPLE happy."

Let's embrace it, because one culture's 'unlucky,' might just be another culture's 'lucky.' And depending on the individual, even both or neither. Definitely no wrong answer here.

Six Degrees Of Jack

Many times, sprinkled between getting forms filled out, are casual conversations about our clients' friends and neighbors living here in Chino Hills.

It's not unusual for me to know some of them. My partner John, who has seen that quite a few times, said,

"You know, there's this game from way back called 'Six Degrees of Kevin Bacon,' where almost everyone in the TV and movie industry can be shown to have some connection with Kevin Bacon. We could probably have something like 'Six Degrees of Jack' around Chino Hills!"

* * *

Thanks, John. You inspired me to buy myself an after-Christmas Christmas present. Found an old set on eBay.

Despite being a long-term mindless project, I'm working on the rules of my game, making sure it's weird, funny and actually playable.

If you've played the game, and have a suggestion or two on how I can adapt it, drop me a line at jack@91709jack.com!

To follow the currently VERY non-existent progress of this project: Jackddd.com/game

November 16

When Hands Deserve More Than A Hand

This is a fitting tribute to a grand lady on a Mother's Day, or any other day. Arthritis, toil and time have taken their toll on her hands.

They have raised children, helped parents, lovingly served a husband for over 50 years, volunteered in church and community. Cooking, cutting, cleaning, caring and most likely everything in between.

In short, a beautiful pair of hands attached to a heart that loves.

So to all our favorite ladies, mothers, wives, sisters, aunts and grandmas out there, a wonderful Mother's Day to you EVERY DAY.

* * *

Actually, S, the lady whose hands these are, also has an edgy sense of humor. The sparkly nail polish on just the ring fingers gave that away, right?

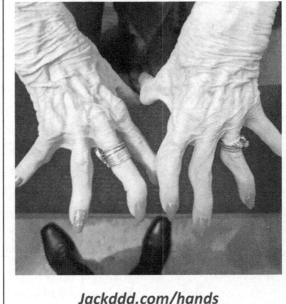

Jackddd.com/hands

November 19

Joyride

After pushing an inexpensive golf bag carrier up a very steep hill where I was the battery, I decided to splurge and ordered a motorized model, with super thick solid rubber tires. The McGyver spirit continues to serve my purposes.

Aside from a big file box, assorted lights, hands-free doodads, hidden diving weights, and of course, an umbrella, it can even sport some seasonal or random ornaments.

The latest tweak was to install an iron basket, to possibly hold goodies or some other thing in the future. Would it hold up?

Cooper, our official mascot, was sitting nearby. And he looked

like just the RIGHT size.

Since my wife wasn't home and nobody was looking, why not?

So in he went, and that's the closest thing he'll ever experience to a ride in the Magic Kingdom.

Disclaimer: No pets were hurt during filming of this video at Jackddd.com/joyride

November 20

I Made That

There's no shortage of incredible talent in our city of amazing people.

"What is THAT?" I asked.

"Oh, I made that. Come on in. Let me show you," B said rather nonchalantly.

"THAT" was a pretty big Maleficent – complete with glowing eyes, smoke out of its mouth, and endless painstaking details. The whole thing was built from scratch.

The picture does NOT do it justice.

* * *

Ridiculously awesome, B! THANKS for sharing with me.

Jackddd.com/dragon

By Bed, By Head,
And I Don't Remember What I Read

K told me he really enjoyed reading the *Ding Dong Diaries*.

"I put it right next to my bed, to enjoy some light reading before going to sleep."

Apparently, not a good idea.

His laughter prevented his wife from sleeping. Oops.

*

In another home, C & T proudly let it be known my book was sitting on the coveted shelf space of their toilet bowl tank.

The first time around, they were racing to see who'd finish first, toilet paper squares marking their progress. Clean ones.

They'd also know someone was likely thumbing through the *Ding Dong* book if they heard laughs from the loo.

*

What surprised me were those of you who kept my book in your CARS. Stumped, I had to ask.

"Oh, when I pick up the (grand)kids every day, I get a few minutes to read a few pages. The next day, since I don't remember what I read yesterday, it's all new to me again!"

P.S. If your copy has too much coffee, ketchup or milk tea on it, let me know. FREE replacement (Chino Hills only, please!)

December 1

Big Dog

After consistently investing the hardest efforts year after year, we can fairly say we've had the privilege of achieving very significant production numbers. We really appreciate your very encouraging and supportive kudos.

"Hey, Jack, congrats on the killer production," or,

"Well, well, well. Guess who's the 'Big Dog'?"

While I may appear to have a big head, it's not because it's filled with pride, but because I was born with one.

God makes sure it stays in check, thanks to my wife, and the dust-licking He allows me to experience every now and then.

But after I met Khan, who's got more hair than me, weighs more than me, and has a tongue that's big enough to cover most of my face, he showed me who's the 'Big Dog!'

And inside that big dog, is a big, lovable heart.

P.S. I didn't forget you, little Sophie!

Jackddd.com/bigdog

T_C_ SHELL
SH_CKED

When I caught L at the door, it was a quick "Hello!" and off she went back in the house.

Absolutely nothing wrong with that. Happy to get that all the time.

She called me two days later, saying,

"Hey Jack, I didn't mean to be so short with you the other day. I was frying some taco shells!" she started.

"L, no worries. What are you talking about? Nothing like that even crossed my mind," I assured her.

"I actually spent the next two hours reading your book. You are such a good person."

Now I'm shocked, and I didn't know what to say.

* * *

L, you and M have been nothing but kind and welcoming from day one. For that alone, I'll always be grateful. Your very kind words have stumped me.

I've come to an honest awareness of the ease and willingness of how I accept insults, much more so than a graciously given compliment.

P.S. Vowels are free today.

Answer: TACO SHELL SHOCKED

December 13

Go For It!

You'll NEVER guess what this cute little thing is.

While chatting with M, his daughters run over and proudly show off their new pet in a pink pail - MINGUS!

Not a puppy, not a hamster or even a guinea pig. Not a fat mouse or rat. Looked like a fat bunny with no ears. I had NO idea what it was, but it was really cute.

Not sure how many times they begged their dad to let them keep it, but he finally said,

"GOPHER" it.

Thanks to the internet, the girls put him in an aquarium. Unfortunately, they put too much sand and this little critter decided to go for it and escaped! Oh well.

* * *

My wife & girls thought it was adorable...until I told them what it was.

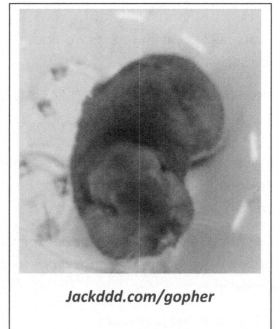

Jackddd.com/gopher

What You Doin'?

Visiting with D, a young lady across the street calls out to me,

"Are you Jack? My parents want to sell their home. Could you please stop by later when you're done?"

They were the only family I never met over these many years.

After getting introduced to G & M, and their son G, and A, their daughter who called me over, they said,

"Oh, we know who you are. We just never got around to answering the doorbell. We've seen you many times. We know the neighbors know who you are too."

M took both my hands, looked me in the eyes, and said, "We feel we can trust you. And I'm very comfortable with you."

* * *

G & M, THANK YOU so much. Just as we got to meet your beautiful family, we had to say "Goodbye!"

*

On occasion I've been told, "That was very kind of you, Jack. I saw what you did." What? How? I don't recall seeing anyone.

You never know who's watching, especially when you least expect it. I've heard "character" defined as "who we are when no one's looking." I'd say it's "who we are when we THINK no one's looking," because there's always someone, or Someone who will WATCH you doin' something.

December 13

Happy Colors

Over the years, J always had one health issue after another.

I can still imagine her slowly coming to the door (she told me she was home all the time, just took a few minutes to get there, and that I should wait).

The front door swings open, J greets me, her smile ignoring the pesky tube to a portable oxygen tank tethered to her side.

*

Meeting at her home after she passed away, something captivated me, and I had to ask her son, G, what they were.

"During the last few months, Mom would get bored. Good thing the caretaker loved to paint, and got her into it."

Seeing them that first time gave me a shot of vitamin JOY, a fitting expression of her vibrant life lived well.

* * *

*J, THANK YOU for leaving these pint-sized explosions of color that allow us a peek into the vivid windows of your soul! PLEASE GO TO **Jackddd.com/colors** TO SEE THIS IN COLOR!*

To the caretaker, you are my HERO!

Accidental DISCOvery

"What is THAT thing?"

It's just a golf bag carrier that became an unconventional solution to relieve my back pain. Nothing more.

Then a whole bunch of you started smiling and laughing, suspicious stares even giving way to snickers.

"You know these times we live in, Jack. So thank you. It's ridiculous for sure, but you crack me up! You made my day. Just keep being you."

The Jackbrella is an ongoing reflection of my practical, creative and unexpected sides. Never thought mashing up disco lights to an umbrella would be a spectacular and happy accident! (Don't take my word for it. Check it out below.)

Love the many ideas from many of you, like the bike lights. A few want cold beer and tacos, or the ice cream truck jingle WITH a cooler full of iced goodies. Now about that Porta Potty...

Hope this little video at *Jackddd.com/disco* brightens up your day. Or night.

December 15

Missing Dog Alert

Love how some have used my car as a bulletin board of sorts. Why text when you can scribble a note and stick it on my car?

(Except the one where an agent angrily reminded me it was HER territory. Even though she doesn't live there anymore.)

But this made me sad. M asked if I had seen their little K as I made my rounds.

That night, I had a crazy idea. I was going to be in M's neighborhood for a few days, so why not?

With each passing day, heading into Christmas, they never gave up hope. Almost 2 WEEKS later, they were happily reunited when someone from another city saw their flyers!

* * *

Jackddd.com/missing

If you ever need a giant neighborhood sign for a missing pet (or spouse), just ask. I can whip out a BIG one.

Jackmobile & Jack, at your service.

P.S. The Queen of Chino Hills Missing Dogs is the one and only Laura Leland Montague. Look for her on Facebook.

K ▶ Chino
Hills Connections
Sun at 3:51 PM ·

As my family and I were out walking our neighborhood today looking for our lost pup K we came upon this car parked near our house. The owner, realtor, Jack Soliman, had stopped by yesterday and learned our pup was missing. This gentleman Jack, then took it upon himself to print a car-sized poster of our missing dog and park it for our community to see. My family and I are beyond touched by this powerful act of kindness. My family thanks you Jack, from the bottom of our hearts. 🖤
#thankyoujack #91709jack.com #kindness

> *WARNING: QR Scan RATED PG – necessary positioning of a finger.

What Obscene Gesture?

Your variety of hand motions greet me all over town – from the handshake, wave, "shhhh" (someone's sleeping), the index finger pointing to the phone, a tap, to even a hug.

Wasn't prepared for this one, as Y welcomed me with her signature 1,000-watt smile, colorful garb, and news that she had recently injured her finger in the kitchen.

And there it was, like a knight suited in armor, one of her fingers wrapped in a shiny metal cocoon.

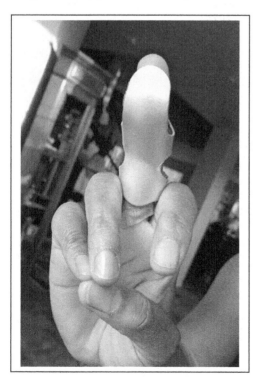

"Hi, Jack! Despite how it looks, it's a medical procedure."

Jackddd.com/finger

Thankfully Y has fully recovered and is back to cooking and waving with all five fingers!

P.S. Not long after, one of her friends badly injured her thumb. Showed her the picture without hints, and she knew who.

December 18

Kept Your Flyer For A Long Time

"Hi Jack. My name is P. Been a broker for over 30 years."

At that point, I usually expect them to say, "I know you guys do a lot in Chino Hills. Got a listing coming up, keep it in mind."

Of course we're happy to. But this call was a little different.

"Kept your flyer for a long time. Already did my research on you. Very impressive. Let's keep things simple. You don't have to explain. Have a rental in Chino Hills. Listing is yours. When can we meet?"

It's almost funny when they just ask for the contracts, and sign away. If there's anyone who would know where all the blanks are, it'd be us agents and brokers!

Some of them have literally left on vacation, or moved away early to their next home, leaving us in charge of everything.

* * *

John & I appreciate every one of you who have trusted us to sell your home. But to receive calls from fellow licensed agents and brokers, who hire us to list their home – is to be honored and humbled at the same time.

Our deepest GRATITUDE to our fellow professionals, for your trust and concrete endorsement of what we have continually worked so hard to achieve.

What's the PENalty?

Nothing unusual about my visit with R & T.

Not until I got to the next door.

"Where's my pen???"

Like a detective I retrace my steps. But I don't find it on the sidewalk. Not in my pocket, or in my man purse. (Don't laugh.)

Heading back to R & T's front door, something catches my eye.

Not only did I see my pen, I also catch the culprit. Very impressed with how my pen was stolen. And the pickpocket didn't even move.

jackddd.com/tree

A bush stole it. Should I impeach? Or just bring the young plant to the courtyard, before a jury of his pears?

The crime? Why, TREEson, of course!

* * *

Many joke about California being a bowl of cereal, a land of nuts, fruits and flakes. Good luck finding evidence of me as a flake. But as a nut or fruit? Guilty for sure.

December 30

Which Of My Friends Don't You Know?

There's someone in town who makes sure I'm up to date on many things Chino Hills.

"Do you know so-and-so?" she'd ask.

More often than not, it would be someone I actually know. To which she'd jokingly end with,

"Well, which of my friends don't you know, Jack?"

On this one particularly heavy month, she phoned me three times in a row, each call relaying news that people we both knew had just passed away.

Flabbergasted I knew the families who had lost loved ones, she still fired her usual question, with a twist, that only her wry sense of humor could cough up in a moment like this:

"Jack, which of my DEAD friends don't you know?"

followed by a hearty laugh.

My goodness.

I laughed too, but I needed to pause to make sure I heard what I thought I heard.

Only you, S.

Only you can get away with something like that.

SOLD! (Updated 12/31/2020)

As of December 31, 2020, in one of the most desirable* areas of Chino Hills, there were a total of **714** properties that were sold over the last **7.5** years.

That represents the hard work of 418 different agents.
The #5 agent sold 9 homes.
The #4 agent sold 12.
The #3 agent sold 33.
The #2 agent sold 34.
The #1 agents sold **128**, with **5** more in escrow.

The agents families chose the most times successfully helped **128** homeowners and counting – that's my partner John & me.

THANK YOU for allowing me to contribute 107 of the 128.

* * *

To every family who interviewed us, thank you.

To every family who gave us a learning opportunity, thank you.

To every successful buyer & seller we represented, Congratulations, and THANK YOU SO MUCH. It will always be a privilege for our John & Jack Team to have taken care of you & your families.

December 31

It's HER Fault

Ding Dong Diaries #1 was really my heart screaming THANK YOU to all of you who showed me way too much kindness and love, packaged in a little book.

It was, and will always be a GIFT to everyone in Chino Hills. Free. Period.

The very first man, Adam, blamed Eve. I'm about to do the same, and blame a woman.

Shortly after I started handing out my book, a very special lady created a little 'problem.'

"Wait, Jack. I can't NOT give you something for your book."

"But, but, it's a GIFT. Like free. Just wanted to THANK YOU. And hopefully get a laugh or two out of you."

Too late. She left me standing at her door, and came back with a $10 gift card. As she places it into my hand, I said,

"Wait - Let me think about what good we can do with this before I even leave."

"I know families. And sometimes, I know they are hurting behind closed doors. EVERY dollar anyone gives me for this book, I'll find a way to give it all away to our families."

Been on my knees when some of your little ones handed me your donation. One walked it into our office. Some of you ambushed my heart when I honestly thought you had mistakenly written in an extra zero. I was not prepared to see gifts of $100. Or even $200.

"Jack, that's not just for the book. It's because it's you we're giving it to, and we know you'll do something good with that."

Charlie had three. But I got an army of angels.

Ana, Andy & Suzi, Angela, Barry & Cynthia, Bill & Lisa, Bill & Sandy, Brent & Leigh, Charlie & June, Chris & Lourdes, Dan & Lynda, Dave & Bella, Dave & Carmen, Don & Donna, Dora, Ed & Cheryl, Edith, George & Cindy, Gil & Liz, Gilbert & Judy, Greg & Becky, Greg & Linda, Jeff & Beth, Jeff & Stacy, Jennifer, Jerry & Sharon, Joe & Sandy, Joe & Yvonne, John & Jeanette, John & Michelle, Jon & Maggie, Kathleen, Kathy, Kazumi, Ken & Audrey, Ken & Chris, Ken & Kimberly, Laurel, Lem & Nancy, Lina, Malik & Sandra, Patrick & Kathy, Paul, Paul & Sara, Pennie, Rich & Loretta, Rick & Sue, Ric & Terry, Rob & Debbie, Ron & Barbara, Roy & Clara & Family, Rudy & Jovita, Saleem & Melanie, Sam & Debbie, Scott & Marci, Sean & Lishya & Family, Sharon, Shirley, Stan & Terri, Steve & Eileen, Tom, Tony & Espie, Tony & Sandy, and Troy & Kathi.

At the end of that first year delivering Ding Dongs, sixty-eight generous Chino Hills families (listed above) gave a total of $1,800 WITHOUT me asking. THANK YOU ALL SO MUCH.

I made out checks to three local families.

(1) A family had a young child, so full of energy, smiles and life, despite a serious health curveball thrown at her.

(2) A retired member of our armed forces, going through the fight of their lives.

(3) A man who faced an aggressive diagnosis with courage, grace and unbelievable gratefulness. Even humor.

It was an honor for me to be the delivery boy for your packets of love on that New Year's Eve afternoon. Included was a note listing the first names of every family who opened their wallets. And big hearts.

While the first two packets were successfully dropped off with no one in sight, I was caught red-handed for the last one. Even though there were smiles all around, there wasn't a dry eye. Looking back, I'm glad it happened. It turned out to be the last time we got to laugh, cry and hug together.

Just in case you'd like to give and be a part of doing something good for our Chino Hills families, and can do so with a big smile, just let me know next we meet. Feel free to text me at 909-262-3132, or email *jack@91709jack.com*. You can wave me down too.

* * *

To you, wonderful lady, I gratefully blame you for this chain-reaction of kindness that is still going.

THANK YOU to every single family who gave from their hearts.

And THANK YOU, Chino Hills.

But Wait, There's...

More. Maybe.

Or...a mistake.

Or...something I really forgot.

So check back once a year.

You never know what will show up.

Even I don't know what might show up.

Jackddd.com/more

NOW I'd really love to hear from YOU.
Anything you'd like to say. Good, bad, anything.

1. Drop me a line at the email above.

 2. Scan the QR code, or just go to *jackddd.com/say*, and you'll be able to DIRECTLY share your thoughts in ONE step.

3. I LOVE pictures. If you'd like to send me one, email or text to 909-262-3132.

4. To support the post office, you can mail it to:
Jack Soliman
13089 Peyton Drive, **Suite C101**
Chino Hills, CA 91709

5. Tell it to my face next time we meet!

Appendix: Welcome To John & Jack's "Fish Market"

*Over $278 Million Closed in Chino Hills

$278,152,435 total volume, representing 320 homes worth $235,967,535 from the listing side, and another 64 homes worth $42,184,900 from our buyers.

Just hard work, day after day, for years.

This is the actual list of EVERY one of the 320 John & Jack homes listed and sold in Chino Hills, starting from April 30, 2013, the day we became partners, all the way to December 31, 2020, for a total production of $235,967,535.

SALE #	DATE	PRICE	ST #	STREET
320	12/30/20	$790,000	16213	Shadow Mountain
319	12/30/20	$910,000	2400	Creekside
318	12/22/20	$980,000	14431	Spring Crest
317	12/15/20	$800,000	16158	Cypress Point
316	12/16/20	$785,000	16241	Phidias
315	11/24/20	$800,000	14797	Maplewood
314	11/24/20	$925,000	3375	Tulip
313	11/23/20	$788,000	2827	Hawk
312	11/17/20	$970,000	14376	Ashbury
311	11/10/20	$950,000	2648	Macadamia
310	11/09/20	$940,000	2157	Deer Haven
309	10/28/20	$750,000	16210	El Dorado

308	10/16/20	$838,000	2461	White Dove
307	10/13/20	$800,000	13587	Seinne
306	10/13/20	$720,000	14650	Bueno
305	10/01/20	$665,000	13625	Running Springs
304	09/29/20	$1,000,000	13462	Montserrat
303	09/17/20	$820,000	2315	Avenida Cabrillo
302	09/16/20	$710,000	2113	Rancho Hills
301	09/09/20	$665,000	2139	Paseo Grande
300	09/09/20	$925,000	2270	Olympic View
299	09/01/20	$684,000	15880	Sedona
298	09/01/20	$849,999	15043	Avenida Compadres
297	08/26/20	$862,500	5675	Avenida De Portugal
296	08/18/20	$725,000	5666	Sorrel Hills
295	08/02/20	$829,250	2316	Monteverde
294	08/02/20	$915,000	6131	Geanie
293	07/30/20	$850,000	5163	Copper
292	07/21/20	$792,500	17310	Eastview
291	07/21/20	$755,000	15000	Avenida Compadres
290	07/13/20	$675,000	2794	Pointe Coupee
289	07/09/20	$833,000	2465	Brookhaven
288	06/29/20	$808,000	2799	Olympic View
287	06/23/20	$1,080,000	4960	Highview
286	06/22/20	$555,000	6332	Viola
285	06/22/20	$800,000	2582	Diamond
284	06/10/20	$750,000	3080	Sunrise
283	06/01/20	$920,000	2360	Eaglewood
282	05/27/20	$580,000	3111	Oakview
281	05/15/20	$405,000	15569	Ethel
280	05/04/20	$855,000	2441	Brookhaven
279	04/20/20	$547,500	15495	Oak Springs
278	04/20/20	$985,000	2361	Olympic View
277	04/14/20	$937,000	16243	Promontory
276	03/30/20	$385,000	3527	Terrace
275	03/17/20	$960,000	13317	Jerome

274	01/24/20	$812,000	6204	Park Crest
273	01/19/20	$717,500	3085	Windemere
272	01/09/20	$385,000	4526	Brookview
271	01/07/20	$548,000	15070	Beechwood
270	12/24/19	$908,000	1674	Rosemist
269	12/16/19	$715,000	2936	Ridgecrest
268	12/12/19	$665,000	13646	Brandy
267	11/25/19	$690,000	15346	Morningside
266	11/04/19	$815,000	2798	Avenida Marguerite
265	10/29/19	$700,000	15503	Feldspar
264	10/30/19	$890,000	1535	Falling Star
263	10/21/19	$532,000	18036	Arroyo
262	10/04/19	$815,000	2372	Creekside Run
261	10/04/19	$798,000	13754	Evening Terrace
260	09/20/19	$819,900	16262	Van Gogh
259	09/12/19	$619,000	2096	Villa Del Lago
258	09/13/19	$815,000	1944	Rancho Hills
257	08/28/19	$876,000	17393	Park
256	08/21/19	$810,000	2018	Rancho Hills
255	08/14/19	$780,000	6001	Park Crest
254	08/14/19	$990,000	6139	Geanie
253	07/29/19	$720,000	14144	Deerbrook
252	06/28/19	$899,900	13630	Nimes
251	06/25/19	$818,000	14164	Wildrose
250	06/21/19	$820,000	2297	Wandering Ridge
249	06/18/19	$800,000	2148	Camino Largo
248	06/17/19	$897,000	1634	Vista Del Norte
247	06/03/19	$885,000	16158	Crooked Creek
246	05/17/19	$842,000	13860	Woodhill
245	05/08/19	$875,000	16311	Sisley
244	05/02/19	$690,000	14530	Terrace Hill
243	05/01/19	$370,000	14689	Moon Crest
242	04/29/19	$860,000	14276	Elm Wood
241	04/22/19	$700,000	2970	Buckhaven

240	04/23/19	$715,000	17413	Kelsey
239	04/20/19	$970,000	1564	Rancho Hills
238	03/30/19	$780,000	1879	Foxgate
237	03/26/19	$758,800	2484	Via La Mesa
236	03/26/19	$999,999	16156	Promontory
235	03/20/19	$925,000	14236	Brook Hollow
234	03/08/19	$720,000	6164	Park Crest
233	03/08/19	$690,000	15048	Calle La Paloma
232	03/06/19	$850,000	16623	Sagebrush
231	02/26/19	$510,000	14693	Lobelia
230	02/19/19	$850,000	15081	Avenida De Las Flores
229	02/13/19	$750,000	1864	Berryhill
228	02/06/19	$736,000	14132	Deerbrook
227	01/31/19	$790,000	14270	Alder Wood
226	01/07/19	$392,000	3240	Southdowns
225	12/18/18	$900,000	14942	Avenida Anita
224	12/15/18	$775,000	2396	Wandering Ridge
223	12/06/18	$777,777	13156	San Rafael
222	11/21/18	$670,000	13083	San Rafael
221	11/15/18	$685,000	15041	Camino Del Sol
220	11/14/18	$912,000	2820	Olympic View
219	11/14/18	$860,000	13054	Rimrock
218	11/05/18	$699,000	3084	Sunrise
217	10/26/18	$740,000	13461	Parkview
216	10/24/18	$800,000	5154	Picasso
215	10/03/18	$900,000	2224	Avenida Las Ramblas
214	10/02/18	$840,000	16376	Sisley
213	10/01/18	$730,000	14680	Deep Creek
212	09/24/18	$900,000	6003	Kylie
211	09/06/18	$990,000	16015	Ranch House
210	09/05/18	$779,000	13581	Meadow Crest
209	09/04/18	$825,000	3237	Richele
208	08/23/18	$785,000	2261	Monteclaro
207	08/09/18	$750,000	13597	Anochecer

206	08/08/18	$770,000	14862	Summit Trail
205	08/01/18	$730,000	1652	Mill Stream
204	07/24/18	$770,000	15345	Georgetown
203	07/19/18	$775,000	1455	Glen Pines
202	06/11/18	$865,000	13762	Vista Grande
201	06/05/18	$865,000	1690	Diamond Valley
200	05/21/18	$906,000	13267	Gemstone
199	05/14/18	$725,000	3083	Sundance
198	05/11/18	$762,000	5047	Stone Ridge
197	05/10/18	$1,068,000	2242	Woodhollow
196	04/30/18	$830,000	14025	Ravenwood
195	04/25/18	$799,888	1916	Rancho Hills
194	04/24/18	$830,000	13594	Seinne
193	03/30/18	$710,000	3411	Royal Ridge
192	03/30/18	$1,098,800	15992	Ranch House
191	03/20/18	$480,000	4018	Bayberry
190	02/27/18	$614,000	3253	Oakridge
189	02/27/18	$690,000	2132	Sun Ridge
188	02/12/18	$890,000	15166	Palisade
187	01/11/18	$790,000	13658	Brandy
186	01/05/18	$750,000	15035	Camino Del Sol
185	01/08/18	$850,000	14348	Golden Crest
184	12/21/17	$725,000	17358	Park Crest
183	12/19/17	$841,000	3291	Royal Ridge
182	12/08/17	$805,000	14424	Muscadine
181	11/30/17	$835,000	15052	Avenida De Las Flores
180	11/28/17	$730,000	3126	Royal
179	11/27/17	$758,000	2982	Buckhaven
178	11/20/17	$995,000	1643	Rainbow Knoll
177	11/15/17	$860,000	16122	Promontory
176	11/07/17	$702,000	3374	Ridge Pointe
175	11/06/17	$731,888	15059	Avenida Del Monte
174	11/07/17	$705,000	16555	Celadon
173	10/27/17	$818,000	2332	Wandering Ridge

172	09/27/17	$1,050,000	13869	Woodhill
171	09/06/17	$683,000	2453	Monte Royale
170	08/18/17	$820,000	15035	Calle La Paloma
169	08/17/17	$800,000	2476	Paseo Del Palacio
168	08/14/17	$769,000	15080	Avenida Del Monte
167	07/06/17	$525,000	5956	Meadowood
166	06/29/17	$899,800	14850	Summit Trail
165	06/29/17	$890,000	2429	Pheasant Run
164	06/27/17	$738,000	14743	Sleepyglen
163	06/27/17	$840,000	14316	Ashbury
162	06/20/17	$775,000	16139	Crooked Creek
161	06/19/17	$820,000	16685	Quail Country
160	06/02/17	$799,800	14965	Forest Spring
159	06/02/17	$835,000	2390	Paseo Del Palacio
158	05/30/17	$605,000	5939	Crestmont
157	05/30/17	$885,000	2423	Olympic View
156	05/19/17	$828,000	16318	Gainsborough
155	04/29/17	$815,000	1727	Vista Del Norte
154	04/27/17	$829,000	6127	Park Crest
153	04/22/17	$665,000	2175	Hedgerow
152	04/14/17	$522,000	6725	Ranchwood
151	04/17/17	$680,000	13298	Stone Canyon
150	04/03/17	$740,000	1769	Vista Del Norte
149	03/24/17	$800,000	14894	Avenida Anita
148	03/14/17	$746,000	2160	Camino Largo
147	03/14/17	$656,000	2883	Hawk
146	03/07/17	$918,000	2310	Madrugada
145	03/06/17	$785,000	16630	Sagebrush
144	02/07/17	$590,000	2624	Chalet
143	02/07/17	$510,000	15874	Tern
142	01/24/17	$655,000	3026	Sundance
141	01/12/17	$842,000	2435	Brookhaven
140	01/10/17	$725,000	14172	Heathervale
139	11/09/16	$1,130,000	15937	Ranch House

138	10/05/16	$345,000	4115	Valle Vista
137	10/05/16	$920,000	1892	Foxgate
136	10/05/16	$825,000	15248	Calle Lomita
135	09/28/16	$800,000	14284	Laurel Wood
134	09/28/16	$731,200	16377	Cadmium
133	09/21/16	$900,000	16203	Cadmium
132	09/16/16	$699,800	13770	Evening Terrace
131	09/15/16	$745,000	1751	Vista Del Norte
130	09/12/16	$750,000	13539	Pageantry
129	09/08/16	$580,000	5862	Ridgegate
128	08/24/16	$832,000	2359	Spring Meadow
127	08/11/16	$692,000	5997	Natalie
126	08/04/16	$620,000	3543	Hillsdale Ranch
125	07/31/16	$535,000	15249	Aqueduct
124	07/29/16	$740,000	16561	China Berry
123	07/25/16	$818,000	2527	Olympic View
122	07/17/16	$925,000	14245	Sapphire Hill
121	06/28/16	$733,000	14278	Alder Wood
120	06/22/16	$730,000	1876	Foxgate
119	05/13/16	$700,000	14227	Parkside
118	05/09/16	$785,000	14878	Avenida Anita
117	05/05/16	$590,000	2949	Steeple Chase
116	04/28/16	$815,000	13617	Palmetto
115	04/11/16	$699,000	2323	Avenida Cabrillo
114	03/31/16	$677,000	3369	Royal Ridge
113	03/25/16	$425,000	3985	Hickory
112	03/25/16	$620,000	2252	Hedgerow
111	03/21/16	$649,800	14764	Foxwood
110	03/14/16	$665,000	3208	Willow Hollow
109	03/02/16	$670,000	1984	Vista Del Sol
108	03/01/16	$740,000	3074	Sunny Brook
107	02/16/16	$768,000	2136	Camino Largo
106	01/15/16	$930,000	14399	Auburn
105	01/04/16	$613,000	13860	Shady Knoll

104	12/22/15	$235,000	13133	Le Parc
103	12/18/15	$440,000	3882	Willow
102	12/04/15	$495,000	4000	Rosebay
101	12/02/15	$585,000	13328	Eagle Canyon
100	12/01/15	$740,000	16375	Sisley
99	11/23/15	$760,000	12899	Sundown
98	11/07/15	$729,800	2248	Wandering Ridge
97	10/30/15	$658,000	2022	Big Oak
96	10/23/15	$785,000	2638	Norte Vista
95	10/23/15	$768,500	13941	Falcon Ridge
94	10/13/15	$682,000	2278	Camino Largo
93	10/09/15	$650,000	3542	Glen Ridge
92	10/02/15	$705,000	1967	Deer Haven
91	09/29/15	$625,000	15163	Palisade
90	09/25/15	$930,000	15177	Via Maravilla
89	09/10/15	$658,000	15665	Pistachio
88	09/13/15	$665,000	13920	Valley View
87	09/09/15	$815,000	16758	Tamarind
86	09/02/15	$539,000	3366	Royal Ridge
85	09/03/15	$465,000	5958	Ridgegate
84	08/14/15	$609,888	4322	Saint Andrews
83	07/27/15	$645,000	14026	Plum Hollow
82	07/16/15	$845,000	1428	Rancho Hills
81	07/10/15	$570,000	15982	Oak Hill
80	07/01/15	$675,000	14101	Deerbrook
79	06/23/15	$699,000	3320	Ridge Pointe
78	06/18/15	$669,000	17396	Jessica
77	06/13/15	$529,800	3244	Oakleaf
76	06/03/15	$815,000	1736	Morning Terrace
75	05/27/15	$665,000	3148	Skyview
74	05/26/15	$690,000	15888	Madelyn
73	05/20/15	$550,000	2304	Avenida La Paz
72	04/20/15	$735,000	13577	Monte Royale
71	03/06/15	$718,000	15733	Sleepy Oak

70	03/03/15	$759,000	2453	Pheasant Run
69	02/11/15	$589,000	2165	Wild Flower
68	01/22/15	$678,000	6200	Natalie
67	01/15/15	$770,000	1522	Rancho Hills
66	12/28/14	$664,500	2165	Monteverde
65	12/19/14	$678,888	13901	Hearth Stone
64	12/18/14	$593,000	6487	Via Del Prado
63	12/16/14	$508,500	16103	Spaulding
62	12/15/14	$550,000	2539	Wandering Ridge
61	12/05/14	$485,000	15861	Sprig
60	11/29/14	$562,500	14042	Sweet Grass
59	11/09/14	$515,000	4343	Jasmine Hill
58	10/24/14	$740,000	13831	Monteverde
57	10/24/14	$425,000	6353	Sunny Meadow
56	10/10/14	$498,800	14775	Velvet
55	10/10/14	$450,000	3933	Bayberry
54	10/03/14	$740,000	2323	Quail Glen
53	09/24/14	$460,000	18013	Prairie
52	09/16/14	$725,000	15738	Pistachio
51	09/08/14	$955,000	16090	Promontory
50	09/08/14	$675,000	12891	Rock Crest
49	09/05/14	$800,000	1885	Walnut Creek
48	09/02/14	$690,000	2461	Monte Royale
47	09/03/14	$945,000	15961	Promontory
46	09/03/14	$845,000	16065	Pinnacle
45	09/03/14	$700,000	16744	Carob
44	08/21/14	$425,000	15806	Antelope
43	08/25/14	$697,500	13574	Pageantry
42	08/15/14	$718,000	14114	Sweet Grass
41	08/04/14	$682,000	1990	Deer Haven
40	07/23/14	$689,800	14161	Heathervale
39	07/23/14	$1,050,000	16065	Promontory
38	07/23/14	$675,000	6044	Park Crest
37	07/18/14	$819,000	1666	Rosemist

36	07/18/14	$768,000	14351	Auburn
35	07/08/14	$575,000	3648	Daisy
34	07/07/14	$739,800	13711	Shadow Ridge
33	06/30/14	$706,000	16139	La Quinta
32	06/23/14	$858,000	16729	Sage
31	06/17/14	$612,800	15237	Green Valley
30	06/06/14	$550,000	6484	Coyote
29	06/03/14	$399,000	4034	Bayberry
28	06/03/14	$489,000	2431	Maroon Bell
27	05/21/14	$1,000,000	15979	Ranch House
26	05/13/14	$1,150,000	15944	Promontory
25	05/09/14	$895,000	2411	Brookhaven
24	05/01/14	$875,000	16681	Tourmaline
23	04/09/14	$900,000	5057	Highview
22	04/09/14	$719,000	17445	Jessica
21	04/01/14	$391,000	15869	Deer Trail
20	03/04/14	$666,500	14176	Wildrose
19	01/17/14	$804,000	2284	Meadow View
18	01/14/14	$580,000	15593	Quiet Oak
17	11/07/13	$685,000	13537	Morning Mist
16	10/24/13	$560,000	2316	Wandering Ridge
15	10/23/13	$475,000	2260	Norte Vista
14	09/28/13	$760,000	12873	Sundown
13	09/25/13	$644,900	3271	Royal Ridge
12	09/25/13	$262,500	13104	Glen
11	09/19/13	$650,000	14550	Reservoir
10	09/05/13	$860,000	12884	Fallview
9	08/29/13	$815,000	2423	Olympic View
8	08/29/13	$679,000	13698	Monteverde
7	08/22/13	$483,988	16715	Bear Creek
6	08/15/13	$730,000	2321	Eaglewood
5	07/20/13	$225,000	13115	Le Parc
4	07/16/13	$685,000	13332	Keystone
3	06/07/13	$425,000	16524	Celadon

| 2 | 05/29/13 | $560,000 | 2949 | Steeple Chase |
| 1 | 05/24/13 | $670,000 | 2319 | Monte Royale |

And that's just the sellers.

There were another 64 Chino Hills buyers, for an additional $42,184,900 in successful closings, bringing our Chino Hills totals to $278,152,435.

That's more than a quarter of a BILLION in one city.

It's a rather long list, but we hope you prefer that over a tiny number.

THANK YOU!

About the Author

Jack Soliman is still not a real author, but a real estate agent who lives and breathes one city, Chino Hills. In the last 7½ years, together with his partner John Balsz, they are the highest producing agents in many of the most in-demand neighborhoods in their city.

In one particularly coveted area* of the city, out of 714 homes sold, Jack & his partner John were responsible for 128. Jack contributed 107 of that total. The next agent did 34.

Jack achieved these results through a unique, unconventional but very personal approach to his business, concentrating on the marketing of their clients' properties, with his partner John expertly overseeing the day-to-day activities from start to close, and by the kindness and support of thousands of families, whom he enjoys visiting every chance he has.

He has lived in Chino Hills since 1990 with his family and their dog, Cooper.

Often introduced as "The $100 Million Underdog," Jack has selectively accepted invitations to speak at events and round tables on topics of sales and marketing as his schedule allows. For inquiries of availability to have him at your company, organization or event, please submit a request at this page: *91709jack.com/underdog*.

*Non-custom, built after 1984, $600,000 to $1.2 million, single family homes in an area bounded by Peyton Drive, Chino Avenue, Chino Hills Parkway and Grand Avenue, and its immediate environs, from 7/1/2013 to 12/31/2020. Source: California Regional Multiple Listing Service (CRMLS)

This

is

the

end

of the

Ding Dongs.

If you continue,

you'll be reading

"Get A Perm"

.sdrawkcaB

I highly recommend you start from the Back Cover. You'll get to experience something from my childhood school days, reading Chinese books by flipping pages from left to right. Might feel a little strange, like driving on the wrong side of the street. But you'll get the hang of it.

Page 15, *Get A Perm*

Congratulations!

You have safely completed **"Get A Perm."**

What's NEXT?

Call Jack.

Call Jack.

Call Jack.

Call Jack.

Call Jack.

Call Jack!

909-262-3132

Just kidding. Unless you really want to.

Page 14, *Get A Perm*

Page 13, *Get A Perm*

The Most Important Page

Things can change. Whenever necessary or relevant, we will post major updates. Just scan the QR code, or use the direct link.

91709jack.com/updates

John can be reached at **909-374-6320**, or *john.balsz@gmail.com*

Jack can be reached at **909-262-3132**, or *jack@91709jack.com*

Page 12, *Get A Perm*

Notes & Questions
For John & Jack

Page 11, *Get A Perm*

Friends With Benefits?

The quality of upgrades and repairs depends on WHO does them, just as the selling price of your home can be affected by your choice of a listing agent.

With over 400,000 Californian licensees, it's not unusual that a neighbor, friend or family member is an agent. Choosing can be difficult, until one DECIDES TO CONSCIOUSLY PRIORITIZE THEIR OWN BENEFIT BEFORE ANY AGENT'S FEELINGS.

Here are ACTUAL comments from some Chino Hills families.

"Never again with friends or family! It was difficult to speak our mind, because we felt bad and awkward. We definitely prefer dealing with unrelated, but professional agents."

"They don't even live close by. I picked my specialist for my knee surgery, and I'll pick a local specialist to sell my home."

"We'd rather keep our personal business away from them."

"Look, they don't even speak the language of most of the current buyers – how can they even market to them?"

"We just don't want something bad happening during the transaction to affect our relationship going forward, especially when we have to see each other during the holidays."

"To be blunt, feels like we're doing THEM a favor. When my wife and I sat down, we concluded it's our financial decision, and we should be doing OURSELVES the favor of hiring the most qualified agents who can benefit US."

Page 10, *Get A Perm*

What Upgrades Make You Money? (cont.)

health needs or elderly parents. Even smaller homes that can creatively put in a shower downstairs would benefit.

5. Lifetime warranty paint jobs. It has never been something that any buyer has asked for, or gotten excited about when a home has it. The prohibitive cost in the tens of thousands isn't worth much to a buyer, who normally want THEIR color.

6. Regular paint. Probably one of the BEST investments any one can make. Be careful with darker colors, whether external or inside. Lighter is safer. Faced with the choice of outside OR inside, in general, do the exterior. Or pick and choose areas to save money but spruce up your home inside and out.

7. Windows. You can spend a fortune, but there are less expensive options. The key is to ideally do ALL of it, should you choose to. In general, buyers will see value if EVERY window is replaced, including the odd-shaped and small ones.

8. Flooring. Most buyers WANT one material all throughout, or at least the entire first floor. Almost anything is better than carpet, as no one wants it, especially in high-traffic areas. Wood, and other versatile laminates are most buyers' favorites, followed by tile, especially those that look like wood. Many homeowners choose to stay with carpet, for both comfort and overall lowest cost, and just let the new buyer change it to suit their tastes and needs.

Page 9, *Get A Perm*

What Upgrades Make You Money?

1. Solar. Almost NOBODY wants them. Usually a deterrent, or a so-so perk for the buyer. Lease transfers, potential issues from installing on a thirty year-old roof come up in buyer comments. Unless you're doing it for the environment regardless of financial reasons, DON'T do it. (Unless you're spending well over $600 a month on your average bill, and can reduce your outlay to under $200, no solar lease or purchase would even make mathematical sense, as it would take decades to break even.)

2. Resurfacing kitchen cabinets. Although cheaper than a new kitchen, still expensive. The main issue? It's like spraying new paint on a 30-year-old car. The paint is sparkling, but the vehicle is still old. Buyers usually assign little value, because it is still the original, or because they plan to rip it all out.

3. Stainless steel appliances. Of course, fairly new appliances look and work much better than decades-old ones. Let's just say we've seen buyers give them away for free to their contractors, or toss them. You invested in the shiny new LG line, but some buyers have custom Vikings on the way.

4. PERMITTED downstairs bathroom SHOWER. Especially for a larger home, 2,500 SF or more, this is an improvement that you could significantly increase the value of your home. Most buyers prefer a downstairs room with a shower, for future

Page 8, *Get A Perm*

8. Dry rot or termite. $$ - $$$. If possible, repair areas of significant damage. If minor, leave for buyer's inspector to call out for repair.

9. Deep clean carpet. $$ - $$$. Almost all buyers will take out the carpet, regardless of age. Only replace sections or rooms if you have to. Just need to make it as clean as possible.

10. Pool. ???. If possible, repair major or obvious issues, as this will stop buyers. At least get an estimate.

11. Paint. $$$ - $$$$. We'll help you minimize. Sometimes, all it takes is a fresh coat on the outside TRIM. Curb appeal is a very significant factor in many ways.

If we had to further simplify these tips into ONE as a guiding principle to keep in the back of your mind no matter what you do, remember these three words:

MOVE-IN READY.

Not remodeled, nor renovated. Just move-in ready. Answer this question: If you had to rent it out the next day, what must you do?

There may be exceptions in your SPECIFIC case. Every home and situation is different.

Feel free to contact us at 909-262-3132 for any questions. And as always, no pressure, no bugging, and no irritating drip campaigns. Ever.

Page 7, *Get A Perm*

The Top 11

Let's keep this simple. Our "Greatest Hits" list.

1. Declutter. $0. Move as much to the garage. For the upstairs, move as much to the SMALLEST bedroom. On surfaces like tables, mantels and shelves, leave one, or at most two items.

2. Move BIG furniture. $0. Move away from the main entry way/foyer, main living room, kitchen, downstairs bedroom, master bedroom and MAIN walking paths. Move a few things, not empty your house. Show off your space.

3. Leave pictures on the wall. $0. Usually better, because you don't want to show nail holes.

4. ???. $. Please call or text 909-262-3132 when you're ready. You'll understand why we chose NOT to print these two crucial items.

5. Retouch. $ - $$. If you have the paint to touch up, it goes a long way.

6. Wash windows. $$. If you have LARGE windows, highly recommended. If not, no big deal. At minimum, keep drapes and shutters open to let maximum light in for showing.

7. Front yard. $$. If you have time, seed. If not, sod. Ideal for the backyard, too, but the front is really important.

Page 6, *Get A Perm*

Two Major Exceptions

1. If you are fortunate to have a home renovated at a cost of tens of thousands, or hundreds of thousands of dollars, and you have that ONE bathroom that is 32 years old, we may highly recommend you to bring it up to match the rest of your remodeled home. You wouldn't want that single deterrent from dissuading a buyer from offering a great price. *(May be worth pawning your pets, kids or grandkids for a short time, until escrow closes.)*

2. The advice we share is from a strictly financial perspective. There are many other reasons beyond the financial, such as peace of mind, or the happy continuation of your marriage. Even if you're listing your home in the next few months, and one of you just cannot simply stand another day of the linoleum bathroom floors, spend the money and swap in the travertine. *(Have been told on more than one occasion remodel expenses were way cheaper than a divorce.)*

Page 5, *Get A Perm*

Should You Remodel For SELLING?

The reality TV shows tell you to. Practical and actual experience does NOT show it to be a good return on your time and money. You may break even and sell faster, but more often it's NEGATIVE if done just for selling.

Instead of remodeling, retouching and repairing will get you more bang for your buck.

Paint, if needed. PLEASE choose neutral colors. The finest hue in a shade of green with orange trim is not a good idea.

Repair, especially if it's damaged enough to suggest neglect. The smaller items, leave it for the inspector to call out. Then the buyer feels they have received value when they ask for it, and you fix it later. If major, we'll let you know if you should address it sooner.

Your goal should NOT be to get top dollar, at the risk of NETTING less. Your goal should be to NET the most. We've had sellers who sold for less NETTING more, than a seller who remodeled significantly at the time of sale, who got a HIGHER sale price, but LOST money or barely broke even.

Please call us BEFORE you spend a big chunk, especially if you're doing it for the purpose of selling. Or even if it's a smaller chunk.

Page 4, *Get A Perm*

Get A Perm

We hope you like our perms.

I actually ran out of space.

It was supposed to read, "Get A Permit!"

Kidding aside, like our perms, this is BIG.

If you've done any MAJOR remodel, especially involving any of the following:

- Additional LIVING space square footage (Note: There's a BIG difference between INHABITABLE and NON-INHABITABLE space, even if both are permitted.)
- Moving or removal of a LOAD-BEARING wall

We STRONGLY recommend getting a permit with the city, even if it's after the fact. We can help with contacts.

Question: We don't have a permit, but we used a licensed contractor. Does that take care of it if we can show proof? Answer: No.

Question: Can we sell it as-is? Answer: Yes. Be aware there'll be buyers who may be concerned with insurance, and even potential financing issues.

Question: What's the potential downside to my selling price? Answer: We have seen anywhere from 5% to 10%, case-by-case.

Page 3, *Get A Perm*

DISCLAIMERS

Our recommendations come from actually selling over a quarter of a BILLION dollars' worth of homes in one city, and not from a staged TV show.

This is a short, quick but action-packed guide.

You may not agree with some, or all of what we share. We hope you do not shoot your friendly and hardworking messengers. (That would be John & me.)

There are always exceptions, and we're happy to bring them up as it applies to your specific situation.

There are always challenges, and we always come with solutions and strategies for you.

Take these recommendations with a grain of salt if you are NOT selling. Or plan on staying put for at least next ten years.

In that case, please do and spend whatever makes your heart flutter and puts a smile on your face even AFTER writing the big check.

The interesting middle ground is if you're remodeling, with a conscious eye towards selling in the future. Happy to help.

And in the end, if your mind's made up, no worries. It's your home, your castle. You're King and Queen. I'm only Jack.

P.S. Don't Miss **The MOST Important Page**. You'll Know When You Get There.

Page 2, *Get A Perm*

Thank You

To every family who has supported us in every way, from remembering us, keeping us in mind, asking us a question, depending on us for advice, referring us to your friends and family, giving us learning opportunities, defending us in our absence, trusting us to be your agents as you buy and sell, and welcoming us in your neighborhood, home, and hearts, we will always be grateful to you, and for you.

You are the most "real" part of our real estate careers.

John Balsz & Jack Soliman

The John & Jack Real Estate Team

Chino Hills, California

Page 1, *Get A Perm*

For information, contact Jack Soliman:

jack@91709jack.com

Paperback ISBN-13: 978-0-9985394-2-3
Ebook ISBN-13: 978-0-9985394-3-0
Audiobook ISBN-13: 978-0-9985394-4-7

*For complete details on our $278 Million of Chino Hills sales, please refer to the Appendix in Ding Dong Diaries 2, pages 221 – 231. All production listed under John Balsz.

Joaquinito "JACK" Soliman   CA DRE #01916419
John Balsz   CA DRE #01331827

Made in the USA
Monee, IL
26 July 2021